Essential JavaScript™
for Web Professionals

ISBN 0-13-013056-7

9 780130 130563

90000

Other Books in the Series

- *Essential CSS & DHTML for Web Professionals*
  Dan Livingston and Micah Brown

- *Essential Perl 5 for Web Professionals*
  Micah Brown, Chris Bellew, and Dan Livingston

- *Essential Photoshop 5 for Web Professionals*
  Brad Eigen, Dan Livingston, and Micah Brown

Essential JavaScript for Web Professionals

Dan Barrett
Clear Ink Corporation

Dan Livingston
Wire Man Productions

Micah Brown
Etail Enterprises

Prentice Hall PTR
Upper Saddle River, NJ 07458
http://www.phptr.com

Library of Congress Cataloging-in-Publication Data

Barrett, Daniel J.
   Essential JavaScript for Web professionals / Dan Barrett, Dan Livingston,
Micah Brown.
      p. cm -- (Prentice Hall essential Web professionals series)
   ISBN 0-13-013056-7 (pbk.)
   1. JavaScript (Computer program language) I. Livingston, Dan.
II. Brown, Micah. III. Title. IV. Series.
QA76.76.J39 B37   1999
005.2'762--dc21   99-16801
                                                      CIP

Editorial/Production Supervision: Benchmark Productions, Inc.
Acquisitions Editor: Karen McLean
Cover Design Director: Jerry Votta
Cover Design: Scott Weiss
Cover Illustration: Jean Francois Podevin, from *The Stock Illustration Source, Vol. 5*
Manufacturing Manager: Alexis R. Heydt
Editorial Assistant: Audri Anna Bazlen
Marketing Manager: Dan Rush
Project Coordinator: Anne Trowbridge

Prentice Hall books are widely used by corporations and government agencies for training, marketing, and resale.

The publisher offers discounts on this book when ordered in bulk quantities. For more information, contact: Corporate Sales Department, Phone: 800-382-3419; Fax: 201-236-7141; E-mail: corpsales@prenhall.com; or write: Prentice Hall P T R, Corp. Sales Dept., One Lake Street, Upper Saddle River, NJ 07458.

Printed in the United States of America

10 9 8 7 6 5 4 3 2 1

ISBN 0-13-013056-7

Prentice-Hall International (UK) Limited, *London*
Prentice-Hall of Australia Pty. Limited, *Sydney*
Prentice-Hall Canada Inc., *Toronto*
Prentice-Hall Hispanoamericana, S.A., *Mexico*
Prentice-Hall of India Private Limited, *New Delhi*
Prentice-Hall of Japan, Inc., *Tokyo*
Prentice-Hall (Singapore) Pte. Ltd., *Singapore*
Editora Prentice-Hall do Brasil, Ltda., *Rio de Janeiro*

Contents

v

Introduction

Welcome! This book is something we wish we had when we were first starting out with JavaScript. At that time, there were basically two types of instructional books on the market: 1200-page tomes of seemingly arcane knowledge, and books that were overly simplified and lacking in practical information. Unfortunately, there were no books that were informative and at the same time provided instruction that could be used quickly and effectively in real-world situations.

This book will guide you through JavaScript using examples taken straight from situations that are faced every day during Web site construction. It starts off with simple examples and becomes quite sophisticated with the scripting toward the end of the book. With that said, let's look a little more closely at how this book is laid out and a brief summary of scripting, as well as what JavaScript can and can't do for you.

◆ How This Book Is Laid Out

Chances are that at least some of you picked up this book when your boss called you into his or her office and showed you a Web site that made use of JavaScript. You were then told in no uncertain terms that it was your job to implement the same, or similar, feature on your Web site. "No problem," you respond, while saying to yourself, "I better learn JavaScript and fast!"

This is often how we expand our skills: We are given a job, and if we don't know exactly how to do it, we quickly learn how. In keeping with this real-world model, this book is split into two main projects. For each of the main projects, we will be responsible for creating and/or upgrading the Web site for a fictitious company.

For the first three chapters, we will revamp the homepage for Shelley Biotechnologies, a fast-growing biotech startup. In each chapter we have at least one project that consists of commonly used JavaScript solutions that range from easy to moderately difficult. At the end of each chapter there are more advanced exercises that you can complete on your own to expand your skills. In the second half of the book we will make some much-needed additions to *Stitch Magazine*'s Web site. The examples will be more advanced than those found in the first project, and they will demonstrate some of the powerful things you can do using JavaScript.

The exercises in the chapters are designed to give you a solid foundation in JavaScript on which you can build as you continue to use it. You will find that more often than not there is more than one way to do things in JavaScript—there really are no right or wrong ways to accomplish tasks.

For all of the examples in the book you can go to the companion Web site located at http://www.phptr.com/ essential and download the HTML and images needed to follow along with the exercises.

◆ An Introduction to JavaScript

What Is JavaScript?

For those of you who are new to the world of Web development and may be learning JavaScript in conjunction with HTML, a quick introduction to JavaScript may be in order. JavaScript is Netscape's built-in, cross-platform scripting language. Like HTML, it will work on all platforms.

JavaScript allows you to enhance the functionality of your Web pages by embedding applications directly into your HTML. You can use JavaScript to build applications that range from adding interactivity to your pages to applications that interact with databases. Although Netscape created JavaScript, it will work on most modern browsers, including Microsoft's Internet Explorer (IE). However, IE doesn't directly support JavaScript. IE has its own scripting language—JScript—that supports most of the features found in JavaScript. In the few instances in which the languages differ, those differences are pointed out and a workaround is presented. As these are the two main browsers on the market, the scripts we will be writing will focus on them.

There are two methods that you can use to include JavaScript in your Web pages—client-side and server-side. Both methods share the same basic language sets. This core language defines a base set of objects and features that will work in both client-side and server-side applications. Each method also has its own extended object and feature sets.

Client-Side JavaScript: How It Works

Client-side JavaScript applications are scripts that are embedded directly into your HTML pages and are executed by the user's browser as it loads the page. At least 90% of all the scripts you encounter on the Web fall into this category. Therefore, this is the method that we will use throughout this book.

When the user's browser calls up an HTML page with JavaScript embedded in it, the browser's JavaScript runtime engine interprets the script from the top down, executing statements as it goes.

One of the advantages of using client-side scripting is that the script can detect and make use of user-initiated events, such as changes to a form or the mouse rolling over a particular graphic. The script is then able to use that information to call other parts of the script, and all of this can be done without going back to the Web server and grabbing any more information. Because our scripts are dependent on being interpreted by the user's browser, a few words on the different browsers and how they differ in handling JavaScript are in order.

Browsers and Versions

As stated earlier, IE and Navigator differ slightly in the implementation of their scripting languages. As a programmer, this makes your life a little more difficult: There will be times when a solution will work differently or not at all on different browsers. Wait—it gets worse: As Netscape and Microsoft come out with newer versions of their browsers, the versions of their scripting languages are changing as well. This means that scripts written using new features may not work in an older browser. But don't get too upset—it's not as bad as it seems. All this means is that you will have to take a little extra care in writing and checking your scripts. There are many techniques that you can use to make sure your scripts will work across the board—we will be exploring these techniques and the appropriate times to use them. However, as this book has *JavaScript* in its title instead of *JScript*, we will be concentrating mainly on Netscape's scripting language.

What JavaScript Can and Can't Do

While the applications that you can create using JavaScript are only limited by your imagination, there are several things that you cannot do such as access or control the user's machine. For security reasons, writing to a user's computer is severely limited. You can store data on the user's machine only through the use of a cookie, and even then you are limited to a simple text file. This protects users from scripts that might harm their computers or allow unscrupulous programmers access to personal information.

A security feature called the "Same Origin Policy" also restricts the access of scripts from one origin access to certain properties or files from other locations. For example, if you have a script located at http://www.yoursite.com/test.html and it tries to access certain properties of an HTML page located at http://www.theirsite.com/test.html, the Same Origin Policy will deny your script access. The properties that the Same Origin Policy restricts are shown in Figure I–1.

Objects	Restricted Properties
images	src, lowsrc
document	anchors, applets, cookie, domain, elements, embeds, forms, lastModified, length, links, referrer, title, URL
layer	src
location	All properties except for x and y
window	find

FIGURE I–1 Same Origin Policy restrictions

These are the main restrictions that you will encounter when writing JavaScript applications. We are sure you will find yourself at times trying to use an object or property to do something that can't be done, but those limitations are less restrictions than just a matter of learning the structure of the language.

As you are starting out, if you think of a possible solution that may differ from the examples in the book, give it a shot; you can often stumble upon a solution that others may not have thought of. With all that said, let's get on with the learning.

Acknowledgments

◆ Dan Barrett

I would like to thank the Academy . . . Oh wait, wrong speech. But seriously, I would like to thank my wife Kristin for her support and understanding over the course of my writing this book.

Thanks to my family—my parents Chuck and Judy and my brother Rick—all of whom put up with me having my nose in a book for most of my childhood. I would also like to thank Dan Livingston and Micah Brown for thinking of me when this project came along and Brad Scott for giving this beast its tech review.

Finally, this book could not have been written without the caffeine-laden wonder that is Mountain Dew.

◆ Dan Livingston

We had the good luck to work with Mark Taub and Karen McLean from Prentice Hall on this project. We especially tested Karen's cattle-herding skills, and she remained remarkably patient and focused throughout the process.

I would like to thank my fiancée, Tanya Muller, for her continuing patience and encouragement. I wouldn't have been able to write this book while starting my own business without her by my side. Her support was, and continues to be, invaluable.

I'd also like to thank W. Bradley Scott of Clear Ink for coming up with the idea of using an online fashion magazine as a fictional company. He also acted as technical reviewer, and was generally very helpful.

Finally, I'd like to thank my design mentor, Brad Eigen of MadBoy Productions. He's the Daddy.

◆ Micah Brown

I would like to give special thanks to my wife, Dawn, who has helped me in too many ways to mention. You are my love, my life, and most importantly, my best friend. I dedicate this book to her and our daughter, Ashley Nova, who has yet to be born into this world—we can't wait to meet you!

Also a special thanks to my parents, William and Donna, and my extended parents, Beppe and Joy, for everything they have done for me these last 29 years. I wouldn't be the person I am today if it weren't for them. I will always be grateful for how much you all have taught me through the years and helped me to grow as a person.

Thanks to Mark Taub and Karen McLean for helping Dan and me get this book series out of our brains and onto paper. You are right, this is a little tougher than we had first imagined! Also, thanks to Carl Gorman, my partner in crime at Etail Enterprises (www.etail.com), and my band members, Kelly and Carl from Nitrus, for putting up with me through all of this.

Finally, thanks to my co-authors Dan Barrett and Dan Livingston, as well as all the others who worked on the books in this series. If it weren't for you, I wouldn't be writing this.

About the Authors

◆ Dan Barrett

Dan Barrett works as a programmer and graphic artist for a successful San Francisco Bay Area Web design firm whose clientele includes Hewlett-Packard, Novell, and Pacific Bell. When he is not sitting in front of his monitor working on Web sites, chances are that he is sitting in front of his monitor pursuing his studies in computer animation. He currently lives in California's Silicon Valley with his wife Kristin.

◆ Dan Livingston

Coming from a background in marine biology, Dan Livingston was drawn to Web design in early 1996. His Web sites have since included high-profile clients such as Apple, Pacific Bell, and Novell. His sites have won numerous awards, and have been featured both in design books and on *CNN Prime Time*. His envelope-pushing DHTML site, Palette Man, has received international recognition, as well as "Cool Site" awards from Yahoo!, Macromedia, and *USA Today*. Dan was a Web designer and scripter at the Web design firm Clear Ink before starting his own successful design/user interface company, Wire Man Productions. He continues to produce titles for Prentice Hall's *Essential* series.

◆ Micah Brown

After working in the print industry for several years, Micah Brown started his career with the Web industry back in 1995 as both a programmer and designer. Some of the sites Micah has under his belt are Dr. Laura, Pacific Bell, Amazing Discoveries, and Ascend Communications.

Micah has also been a technical reviewer for Prentice Hall for the last three years for various publications, most notably *Perl by Example* by Ellie Quigley.

Micah is currently a co-owner of Etail Enterprises, a Web consulting firm located in southern California that specializes in bringing companies into this new arena of online advertising.

1 Dynamism and Detection

IN THIS CHAPTER

- Project I: Generating Platform-Specific Content
- Project II: Printing Copyright Information and Last-Modified Date
- Recap
- Advanced Projects

Okay, you've landed the job programming the Web site for Shelley Bio-technologies. At the moment, the site is very static, and your new boss has brought you onboard to bring it up to speed with the competition. Before you begin your work, however, your boss wants you to resolve an issue that has been raised by some people who have been browsing the site. It seems that people who are using Macintoshes are not seeing the text in the same way as people who are browsing the site on a Windows-based machine (see Figure 1–1). Upon further investigation you find out that the font size is displayed differently on the two platforms, and even though the problem isn't the end of the world, the boss is a stickler for details. This looks like a perfect place to start using JavaScript.

Using JavaScript we are able to see what platform and browser are being used to view the site. Now we want to send out the content that best fits that user.

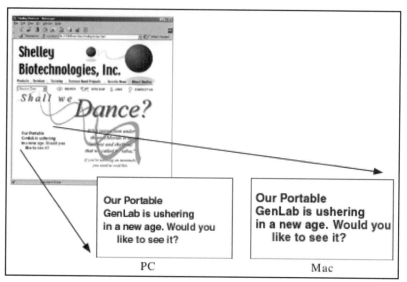

FIGURE 1–1 Font differences on the different platforms

◆ Project I: Generating Platform-Specific Content

After playing around with the existing HTML, you have concluded that, in order for the page to look the same on both platforms, a font size of 2 for the Macintosh and a font size of 3 for Windows machines are required. To solve our problem we are going to need to write the FONT tag dynamically into the HTML, so our script needs to be placed inside the body of the HTML in the spot where the FONT tag would normally reside.

For this first script there are two main parts: First, we must find out what platform the user is on; and second, we need to have the browser dynamically print out the different code needed for each.

Inserting a Script into Your HTML

The first step to writing any JavaScript is to tell the browser that the code you are putting into your Web page is not HTML, but a JavaScript application. Once it knows this it will send the information to the JavaScript runtime engine, which will execute the script. For most scripts we accomplish this by enclosing the scripts in the <SCRIPT> tag.

```
<SCRIPT>
...
</SCRIPT>
```

There are several other ways in which you can embed your scripts into your HTML:

- Specify an external file, which contains your scripts.
- Specify a JavaScript expression as a value for an HTML attribute.
- Embed your scripts within some HTML tags as event handlers.

The <SCRIPT> tag is by far the most commonly used method—we will go over some of the others later in the book when we start using JavaScript with images and forms. If the browser finds JavaScript outside of a <SCRIPT> tag or not used in one of the other methods mentioned previously, your script will be treated as text to be printed on the screen and it won't work.

As new versions of JavaScript come out, there are properties and expressions that are added to the tools available in the language. If you use these new features in your scripts and a system with an older browser loads your script, chances are good that it will receive an error and your script will not work correctly. In order to check for this, we can add an attribute to our <SCRIPT> tag to tell the browser what version of JavaScript we are coding for. When the user's browser gets to the script it will check to see if it supports the version we specify, and if not, it will skip over the script. We do this by using the LANGUAGE attribute of the <SCRIPT> tag.

```
<SCRIPT LANGUAGE="JavaScript1.2">
...
</SCRIPT>
```

The addition to the preceding statement tells the browser that if it does not support version 1.2 of JavaScript, it should not continue with the script. This method will take care of cloaking for JavaScript-capable browsers; however, it is possible that some users are on older browsers that do not support JavaScript at all. You can solve this by putting all of your code in between HTML comment tags, as follows:

```
<SCRIPT LANGUAGE="JavaScript">
<!-- Code after this will be ignored by older browsers
...
// Stop hiding the code here -->
</SCRIPT>
```

Now we know how to put our scripts into our HTML. However, before we get into the script in earnest, an understanding of the hierarchy of JavaScript is in order.

JavaScript Hierarchies

When your browser loads an HTML page, the JavaScript engine automatically creates a set of objects based on the content of your HTML. It keeps these objects in a hierarchy, which can then be used to call on or reference the objects and their properties (see Figure 1–2).

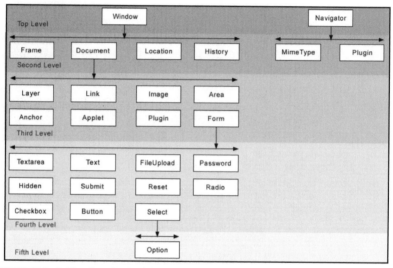

FIGURE 1–2 The JavaScript hierarchy

The WINDOW object is at the top of the JavaScript hierarchy; this object is the actual window in which your browser appears. The descendants of the WINDOW object are its properties and are also objects themselves that can have descendants. For example, if you have an image called product on your page, then product is an object of the type image, but it is also a property of the DOCUMENT object that in turn is a property of the WINDOW object. The understanding of the hierarchy, its objects and properties, is essential to writing applications in JavaScript. A glossary of all the JavaScript objects and their properties is located in Appendix B, "JavaScript Objects."

To reference an object in JavaScript you must call the object itself and all of the objects above it on the hierarchy. Here's an example of how you would refer to the object of our image, `product`:

```
document.product
```

To call on a specific property of an object you follow this same model and just take it a step further down the hierarchy. Calling on the source property of the `product` image looks like this:

```
document.product.src
```

You will notice that the `WINDOW` object was not included as the first object in the preceding examples. If you do not specify a particular window, JavaScript automatically assumes that you are referring to the window in which the document is loaded. The only time that you need to specify the window is when you are trying to access objects that exist in another window or frame. At this point, you should have at least a basic understanding of the JavaScript hierarchy; as we continue with the examples in this book, that understanding will increase.

Platform/Browser Detection

We're now ready to start writing our script. The first thing we need to do is access the `platform` property of the `NAVIGATOR` object—the value of this property will tell us which platform the user is on. We are going to use the value of that property as a test in an `if` statement to determine which font size we want on our page.

An `if` statement is a conditional statement that says if a specific condition is met, go ahead and execute the code that follows; otherwise, skip down to the next statement.

In most cases we are going to be putting our scripts into the <HEAD> of your HTML page. However, when you are dynamically creating text you need to put at least part of the script into the body of your HTML where you want the text to be placed. For this project we will be placing our script in the spot where the text we want to replace dynamically is located in the HTML document. Here is a section of the HTML code that indicates where we will be placing our script.

```
<TR>
<TD>       </TD>

<TD VALIGN="TOP"><BR><BR>
```

```
**** OUR SCRIPT WILL GO HERE ****

<FONT FACE="Helvetica, Arial" COLOR="#000000">
<B>Our Portable
<BR>GenLab is ushering
<BR>in a new age.</B></FONT>
<FONT FACE="Helvetica, Arial" COLOR="#0000FF">
<B>Would you
<BR>    like to see it?</B>
</FONT></FONT></TD>

    <TD>
<BR>       <IMG
SRC="images/h_read.gif" WIDTH=255 HEIGHT=175 BORDER=0
ALT="Read This"></TD>
    </TR>
</TABLE>
```

Now that we know where to put our script into the HTML
code, let's go ahead and insert the first chunk of our script.

```
<SCRIPT LANGUAGE="JavaScript">
<!-- Code after this will be ignored by older browsers

// Assign the platform type to a Variable
var platform = navigator.platform.substr(0,3);

   ...

// Stop hiding the code here -->
</SCRIPT>
```

Let's dissect this first bit of code line by line and figure out what
is going on. First, we put in the opening <SCRIPT> tag as we discussed in the beginning of the chapter. For this script we are only
going to be using code that is supported in all versions of Java-
Script, so we don't need to specify which version we are coding for
in the LANGUAGE attribute of the <SCRIPT> tag. After the <SCRIPT>
tag, we started the HTML comment line, which will hide our code
from nonJavaScript browsers. These first two lines will be the beginning of all the scripts we write, so get used to seeing them.

The third line is a JavaScript comment; as in HTML, you are
able to add notations to your code to help make your scripts easier to follow. There are two ways to insert a comment into your
JavaScript. The first (the method that we are using here) is to start
a line of code with two forward slashes.

```
// Anything on this line is treated as a JavaScript Comment
```

In this method any code that follows the slashes on that single line is treated as a comment, and won't be interpreted as code to be executed. The second method is used when you want to insert a comment that spans multiple lines. To do this, you enclose your comment between these symbols, /* and */. For example:

```
/* This an example of a comment
   that spans multiple lines of code */
```

As we write our scripts we will be using these JavaScript comments to identify each major section of the code and specify its basic purpose.

After we have inserted our comment we can move on to the meat of our script. The fourth line uses the basic assignment operator (=) to assign the value of the platform property to the variable platform.

Several new things are happening on this line of code, so let's break it down and take a closer look at what is going on. First, we are using an assignment operator to set the value of the left-hand operand to be the value of the right-hand operand. We also have things happening on both sides of the operator: On the left-hand side we are creating a variable for the first time. Variables play a very important role in scripting of any sort, and JavaScript is no exception. A variable can be thought of as a container with a user-defined name in which you can store information.

Once you have created a variable you can simply call the name of the variable to access the information it contains, or reassign it new information to hold. The syntax for creating a new variable is as follows:

```
var variablename;
```

On the left-hand side of the operator we are creating a new variable called platform. This variable is now ready to hold the value that is passed into it from the right-hand side of the operator. On the right-hand side, we are performing two actions: First, we are calling on the platform property of the NAVIGATOR object; this property holds a string value that will tell us which platform the user is on. If the user is on a Windows-based machine, the value of navigator.platform will be either "Win32" or "WinNT." If the user is on a Macintosh computer, it will return the value "macintosh."

We are not really interested in knowing which version of Windows the user is running, so it would be great if we could find a way to condense the value returned by Windows-based machines to just the first three characters: "Win." Then, a single value would be assigned to our `platform` variable regardless of which version of Windows the user is running. Luckily, there is a way—it's the second action that we're performing on the right-hand side of the operator. The `substr()` method will return a specified number of characters from any given string. Because we know that the first three letters returned from all versions of Windows are the same, this is perfect for us. The syntax for the `substr()` method is as follows:

```
string.substr(start,length);
```

with `start` being the position of the character you wish to start with, and `length` being the number of characters that you want the method to evaluate. In the preceding line, we are telling the `substr()` method to start at the first character and go until the third. The assignment operator will now put either "Win" for Windows-based machines or "Mac" for Macintosh machines into our `platform` variable.

We now have the information necessary to put in our next piece of code: We will use an `if_else if_else` statement to test the value of `platform`. Let's look at the syntax of this statement.

```
if (condition1)
{
    statements1
}
else if(condition2)
{
    statements2
}
else
{
    statements3
}
```

In the preceding syntax, both `condition1` and `condition2` represent any expression that will return a value of `true` or `false`. If `condition1` is `true`, the JavaScript engine will execute the code contained in `statements1`. If, however, `condition1` is `false`, the JavaScript engine will skip over `statements1` and move on to test `condition2`. If `condition2` is found to be `true`, the engine will execute `statements2`. If it turns out that both `condition1` and `condition2` are `false`, then `statements3` will be executed. The `if` statement is one of the most commonly used structures within JavaScript, and we will be seeing a lot of it throughout the book. With that explained, let's put in the next section of code that contains our if statement.

```
<SCRIPT LANGUAGE="JavaScript">
<!-- Code after this will be ignored by older browsers

      // Assign the platform type to a Variable
var platform = navigator.platform.substr(0,3);


      // If statements testing for which platform the
      // user is on
   if (platform == "Win")
   {
     . . .
   }
   else if (platform == "Mac")
   {
     . . .
   }
   else
   {
     . . .
   }

   // Stop hiding the code here -->
   </SCRIPT>
```

In the if statement in the preceding code, we are telling the JavaScript engine to first look at the value of platform and if it is equal to the string "Win," then execute the statements that follow within the set of curly braces. If the value of platform does not equal "Win," skip down to the else if line that tests the value of platform against the string "Mac." If a match is found there, go ahead and execute the statements below that that are enclosed in curly braces. If no match is found for either "Win" or "Mac," then the if statement will execute the code after the else line.

Notice that we are using the double equal signs (==) to compare the values in our conditions—this is how we do comparisons in JavaScript. If we were to use a single equal sign, it would treat the statement as an assignment operator, thereby resetting the value of platform.

We now have a basic structure for our script, which will detect what browser is being used to view your page. The only remaining part is to insert the code that we want the browser to execute for each of the platforms.

Creating Dynamic HTML from within JavaScript

As it is our goal to have different-sized fonts appear for the different platforms, we need to have the JavaScript write out the <FONT> tag dynamically. There are two statements you can use to write to an HTML document: `document.write()` and `document.writeln()`. They both will print whatever falls between their parentheses; however, `document.writeln()` will insert a line break after it is finished printing. It usually will not matter which method you use, but for our script we will use `document.writeln()` so that if you were to view the source of the HTML page once the code had been printed, it will be formatted for easier reading.

You can use these commands to print out several different types of information. Anything enclosed in quotes within the parentheses will be printed as a string, and you can also put variables or even other JavaScript commands inside and it will evaluate them before printing them. For our purposes, we will print only a string that contains the <FONT> tag. Let's insert the `document` `.writeln()` method into our `if` statements.

```
<SCRIPT LANGUAGE="JavaScript">
<!-- Code after this will be ignored by older browsers

     // Assign the platform type to a Variable
var platform = navigator.platform.substr(0,3);


     // If statements testing for which platform
  if (platform == "Win")
  {
    document.writeln("<FONT SIZE=\"3\">");
  }
  else if (platform == "Mac")
  {
    document.writeln("<FONT SIZE=\"2\">");
  }
  else
  {
     document.writeln("<FONT SIZE=\"3\">");
  }


// Stop hiding the code here -->
</SCRIPT>
```

With that done, if the user is on a Windows-based machine, a <FONT> tag with the SIZE attribute of 3 will print. If the user is on a Macintosh, the attribute will be 2. If neither platform is being used (that is, the user is on a Unix-based machine), then a font size of 3 will print. In our document.writeln statement, you will notice the addition of a backward slash in front of the quotes that surround the numeric value of the FONT SIZE attribute. The slashes are put there to tell the document.writeln statement to actually print the quote instead of treating it as an end quote for the statement. This is known as *escaping a character*; you can use this to have JavaScript treat reserved characters at face value instead of evaluating them.

REVIEWING THE SCRIPT

Congratulations, you are finished with your first script. We now have a script that will deliver different content to users on different browsers. Let's take one last look at the entire script and quickly go over how we accomplished it.

```
<SCRIPT LANGUAGE="JavaScript">
<!-- Code after this will be ignored by older browsers

     // Assign the platform type to a Variable
var platform = navigator.platform.substr(0,3);


     // If statements testing for which platform
  if (platform == "Win")
  {
    document.writeln("<FONT SIZE=\"3\">");
  }
  else if (platform == "Mac")
  {
    document.writeln("<FONT SIZE=\"2\">");
  }
  else
  {
     document.writeln("<FONT SIZE=\"3\">");
  }

// Stop hiding the code here -->
</SCRIPT>
```

Here are the steps we took to create this script:

1. We set up a variable to carry a specific part of the value of the `navigator.platform` object using the `substr()` method.

2. We then used the value of our `platform` variable as a test in an `if` statement to choose which statements we wanted our `if` statement to execute.

3. We used the `document.writeln()` method to dynamically print the proper `<FONT>` tag.

We have been introduced to several new aspects of JavaScript in this first script:

- Inserting scripts into HTML documents.
- Hiding our scripts from nonJavaScript-capable browsers.
- The JavaScript hierarchy.
- Inserting comments into your JavaScript.
- Creating a variable and using an assignment operator to give it a value.
- The use of the `substr()` method.
- The syntax and use of an `if...else` statement.
- The `document.write` and `document.writeln` methods.
- Using the `\` to escape reserved characters.

◆ Project II: Printing Copyright Information and Last-Modified Date

Now that the boss knows that you can dynamically add content to a Web page, he has some other Web-related projects for you: the addition of both the copyright information and the date a page was last modified to the bottom of each page on the site (see Figure 1–3). The addition of the last-modified date is going to be especially helpful in the case of the Shelley Web site. There are many people who make changes to pages on the site and it would be great if there were an easy way to tell if a file had been changed since you last edited it. Like most projects, even though the boss didn't know it could be done 20 minutes ago, it is now a high priority that must be completed ASAP—so let's get started.

FIGURE 1–3 Location of the last-modified date and the copyright information

Introduction of the Last-Modified Property

After a little research into the different properties of the DOCUMENT object, you come across a property that is going to make our script much easier. It seems that we're not the first people to think a last-modified date would be a good idea. Those nice people who created JavaScript included the `lastModified` property to the DOCUMENT object. When a page is loaded and the JavaScript hierarchy is created, the engine goes to the HTTP header and gets the date of the last modification to the page and assigns it to the property. There is one drawback, however: Not all Web servers include this information in the header, so we are going to have to use an `if` statement to make sure we only print it if the value is given. But, beggars can't be choosers, and an extra `if` statement will give us some more practice.

If the Web server doesn't provide a date, then the `last-Modified` property will have a value of 0—we will use this value as our test in our `if` statement. First, let's take a look at the section of HTML code in which we will be putting our script.

```
<TR>
    <TD COLSPAN="3" ALIGN="RIGHT" VALIGN="TOP">
    <FONT SIZE="-2">

    **** OUR SCRIPT WILL GO HERE ****

    </FONT>
    </TD>
</TR>
</TABLE>
</FORM>
</BODY>
</HTML>
```

Now that we know where to put our code, let's start by inserting our <SCRIPT> tags and the HTML comments that will hide our script from older browsers.

```
<SCRIPT LANGUAGE="JavaScript">
<!-- Code after this will be ignored by older browsers
    . . .

// Stop hiding the code here -->
</SCRIPT>
```

The first step in our script is to create and assign a variable the value of the `lastModified` property.

```
<SCRIPT LANGUAGE="JavaScript">
<!-- Code after this will be ignored by older browsers

// Assign the last modified date to the variable lastmoddate
var lastmoddate = document.lastModified;

. . .

// Stop hiding the code here -->
</SCRIPT>
```

Now that we have a variable named `lastmoddate` that holds the value of the `lastModified` property, let's set up an `if` statement to check and see if the `lastModified` property actually contains a date.

```
<SCRIPT LANGUAGE="JavaScript">
<!-- Code after this will be ignored by older browsers

// Assign the last modified date to the variable lastmoddate
var lastmoddate = document.lastModified;

// Create an if statement to test the value of lastmoddate
if(lastmoddate == 0)
{
...
}
else
{
...
}

// Stop hiding the code here -->
</SCRIPT>
```

The `if` statement in the preceding code is very similar to the one that we used in our first script in this chapter; however, it is slightly less complicated in that its structure consists of only `if...else`. Therefore, if `lastmoddate` is equal to 0, then the statements that follow will be executed, and if the value is anything else, then it will skip down to the statements that follow the `else`. Now that we have our `if` statement set up, let's look at what we want to print as HTML.

Dynamically Printing Nonstring Data

In the first script in this chapter, we used the `document.writeln()` method to print a specified string as HTML. For this script, we will be expanding on that to print a combination of string and nonstring data. First, though, we will use the method with which we are already familiar to print the content needed if no date was found in the `last-Modified` property. If this is the case, we will be printing two lines: The first will be a line indicating that the last-modified date is unknown. Next, we will print an HTML line break and the second line, which contains the copyright information.

```
<SCRIPT LANGUAGE="JavaScript">
<!-- Code after this will be ignored by older browsers
```

```
// Assign the last modified date to the variable lastmoddate
var lastmoddate = document.lastModified;

// Create an if statement to test the value of lastmoddate
if(lastmoddate == 0)
{
document.writeln("Lastmodified: Unknown<BR>&copy; 1999
Copyright Shelley Biotech");
}
else
{
. . .
}

// Stop hiding the code here -->
</SCRIPT>
```

With that done we now need to insert the code that will print the content needed if the date was given in the `lastModified` property. As stated earlier, we are going to be heading into slightly new territory as far as the `document.writeln()` method is concerned. So far, we have had the method print only a string; now we are going to use it to print out a combination of string data and the value held by the `lastmoddate` variable. We will accomplish this with the following line of code:

```
document.writeln("LastModified: " + lastmoddate +
"<BR>&copy; 1999 Copyright Shelley Biotech")
```

To combine the different types of data we need to use the concatenation operator (+). This operator will take two or more strings and combine them to return a new string. Even though the variable `lastmoddate` isn't a string itself, the value that it holds is a –string, so this method will work. Therefore, in the preceding line, we are first combining the string `LastModified` with the value held within `lastmoddate`, and then combining that new string with a string that contains an HTML line break and the copyright information. Let's see how this line of code looks in the rest of the script:

```
<SCRIPT LANGUAGE="JavaScript">
<!-- Code after this will be ignored by older browsers

// Assign the last modified date to the variable lastmoddate
var lastmoddate = document.lastModified;
```

```
// Create an if statement to test the value of lastmoddate
if(lastmoddate == 0)
{
document.writeln("Lastmodified: Unknown<BR>&copy; 1999
Copyright Shelley Biotech");
}
else
{
document.writeln("LastModified: " + lastmoddate +
"<BR>&copy; 1999 Copyright Shelley Biotech");
}

// Stop hiding the code here -->
</SCRIPT>
```

REVIEWING THE SCRIPT

The addition of that last line was the final piece needed to complete this script. We now have a script that will dynamically print the last-modified date and the copyright information of all pages in which we place the script. As with all of the scripts in the book, we will take a look at the completed script, how we did it, and what new areas we covered in the process.

```
<SCRIPT LANGUAGE="JavaScript">
<!-- Code after this will be ignored by older browsers

// Assign the last modified date to the variable lastmoddate
var lastmoddate = document.lastModified;

// Create an if statement to test the value of lastmoddate
if(lastmoddate == 0)
{
document.writeln("Lastmodified: Unknown<BR>&copy; 1999
Copyright Shelley Biotech");
}
else
{
document.writeln("LastModified: " + lastmoddate +
"<BR>&copy; 1999 Copyright Shelley Biotech");
}

// Stop hiding the code here -->
</SCRIPT>
```

Here are the steps we took to create this script:

1. We assigned the value of the `document.lastModified` property to the variable `lastmoddate`.

2. We then created an `if` statement to check if the Web server actually passed a last-modified date to the Java-Script engine.

3. We inserted a statement using the `document.writeln()` method that will print a message indicating that the last-modified date is unknown, and the copyright information, if there was no date contained in the variable `lastmoddate`.

4. We wrote a statement that used the `document.writeln()` method to print out a combination of string data and the date contained in the `lastmoddate` variable, along with the copyright information, if a last-modified date was given.

Let's look at the new concepts that we have used in this project:

- The `lastModified` property of the DOCUMENT object.
- How to combine strings and nonstring values with the use of the concatenation operator (+).

RECAP

Well, we have gotten off to a great start with the Shelley Biotech Web site. In a relatively short time we have added two very useful new features to the homepage. As time passes and there are new browsers on the market that handle HTML a little differently, being able to get user information and customize your pages for site visitors is becoming ever more important. The other area that we touched on in this chapter, dynamic creation of content, is an area of JavaScript that has major potential for making the up-keep and maintenance of a Web site more efficient. As we get further into this book, we will see many examples of what we can accomplish using these concepts.

ADVANCED PROJECTS

The scripts in this chapter are fairly simple examples of what you can accomplish with platform/browser detection and dynamic HTML generation. Try using these techniques in the following projects to get a better understanding of the great results you can achieve:

1. Use browser detection to dynamically create pages that are customized to work with specific browser versions.

2. Create a page that will gather all of the information contained in the NAVIGATOR object, and dynamically generate a table that will display that information to the user. (The information gathered from the user's browser and placed in the table is useful as a development tool.)

3. If you have a site where specific content appears on all pages, use the document.writeln() method to print the code, and then save the script in an external JavaScript file. In each page, simply call the external file using the SRC attribute of the <SCRIPT> tag. This will let you update only one file to affect site-wide changes.

2 Image Rollovers

IN THIS CHAPTER

- Project I: Rollover Script
- Project II: Adding Advanced Functionality to Our Rollovers
- Rollover Quirks
- Recap
- Advanced Projects

You've gotten the ball rolling on the homepage and shown that you've got what it takes to get the job done—now your boss wants you to wow him. He is looking to make the site more dynamic and give it a little bit of flash. He has been checking out your competitors' sites and they all have image rollovers—JavaScript rollovers are used to swap an image with a different version of that image when the user moves the cursor over the image. Conversely, when the user moves the cursor off the image, the new image is replaced with the original. This technique is widely used on Web pages, and he feels this is just what your site needs.

The first thing to do is to choose which graphics you want to be affected by the rollovers. The best place for image rollovers on most pages is on the main navigation graphics, and the Shelley Biotech site is no different (see Figure 2–1).

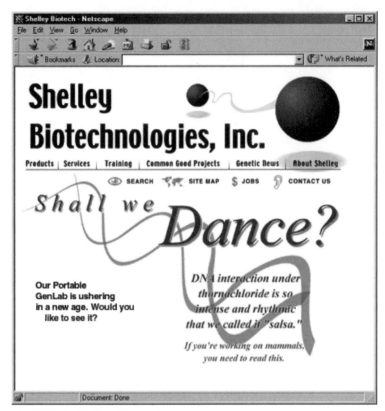

FIGURE 2–1 Shelley Biotech homepage

One of the designers has come up with a great graphic treatment for the rollovers and it's now up to you to implement them (see Figure 2–2). There are three steps to creating an image rollover: define the IMAGE objects, create the function that will do the work, and insert the necessary JavaScript event handlers into your image and anchor tags. First, we'll go over the creation of the IMAGE objects.

◆ Project I: Rollover Script

Creating the IMAGE Objects

Before we get to the actual creation of the IMAGE objects themselves, we must put our <SCRIPT> tag into the HTML page.

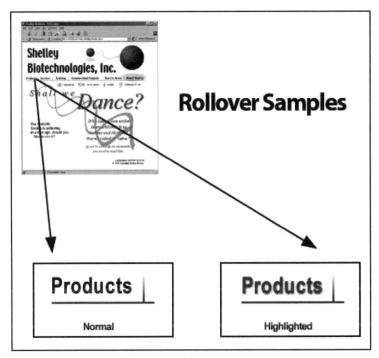

FIGURE 2–2 Image rollover sample

Unlike the scripts in the preceding chapter, we are not looking to print out content within the page, so we are going to put our script into the head of the HTML page.

```
<HEAD>
<SCRIPT Language="JavaScript ">
<!-- Code after this will be ignored by older browsers


. . .

// Stop hiding the code here -->
</SCRIPT>
</HEAD>
```

We now need to cloak for older browsers that don't support the IMAGE object, which is necessary for our rollover script. In the first chapter, we learned how to use JavaScript to gather the browser and platform information. We could use a variation of that method in which we set up several if statements that test for every browser that doesn't support the IMAGE object; however, this would be a lot of work. Fortunately, there is a simpler way. We can test if the user's browser supports rollovers using only a single if statement, as shown in the following lines of code:

```
<HEAD>
<SCRIPT Language="JavaScript">
<!-- Code after this will be ignored by older browsers

    // Creation of the image objects
if (document.images)
{
...
}
// Stop hiding the code here -->
</SCRIPT>
</HEAD>
```

In the preceding lines of code, we used

```
document.images
```

as the condition in our if statement. It will return a value of true if the browser supports the IMAGE object, and a value of false if it does not. By inserting our code within this if statement we are, in effect, cloaking our code from browsers that cannot handle the script.

When an HTML page is loaded, and the browser creates the objects that make up the JavaScript hierarchy, every image laid out on the page is made into an object and put into an array called images. This is the first time we have come across arrays, so let's look at what an array is and, in particular, the images array and how we are going to use it.

You can think of an array as a filing cabinet. Let's say you have a page with four images on it. When the browser reads the HTML file, it moves down the page; and when it reaches the first image it creates an IMAGE object for it and stores it in the first drawer of our filing cabinet. When it reaches the second image, it again creates a new IMAGE object, then puts it into the second drawer of the filing cabinet. This pattern continues until each of the images on the page has its own IMAGE object, which is stored in its own drawer.

When the browser needs to reference an image, it looks in the appropriate drawer. You, too, can reference the array and the IMAGE objects held therein—there are two ways to do this. The first is to reference the location in the array at which the IMAGE object resides. The problem with this method is that if you add an image somewhere on the page, the position of all of the images following it will change. Therefore, you'll have to go through your whole script and make sure an image you were calling didn't move to a different position.

The second method, which we will be using in this script, takes care of this problem. If you specify a NAME attribute in your <IMG> tags, you can then reference that graphic in the array by the name that you have assigned to it. With this method, even if you add other graphics to the page, you will still be able to reference the IMAGE object the same way and your script won't be adversely affected.

There are six navigation images that will be affected by our rollover script, so for each of those images we need to assign a NAME attribute in the <IMG> tags.

```
<A HREF="products/index.html"><IMG SRC="images/
h_products_off.gif" WIDTH="71" HEIGHT="33" BORDER="0"
NAME="Products" ALT="Products"></A>

<A HREF="services/index.html"><IMG SRC="images/
h_services_off.gif" WIDTH="67" HEIGHT="33" BORDER="0"
NAME="Services" ALT="Services"></A>

<A HREF="training/index.html"><IMG SRC="images/
h_training_off.gif" WIDTH="75" HEIGHT="33" BORDER="0"
NAME="Training" ALT="Training"></A>

<A HREF="common/index.html"><IMG SRC="images/
h_common_off.gif" WIDTH="157" HEIGHT="33" BORDER="0"
NAME="Common" ALT="Common Good"></A>

<A HREF="genetic/index.html"><IMG SRC="images/
h_news_off.gif" WIDTH="98" HEIGHT="33" BORDER="0"
NAME="News" ALT="Genetic News"></A>

<A HREF="about/index.html"><IMG SRC="images/
h_about_off.gif" WIDTH="106" HEIGHT="33" BORDER="0"
NAME="About" ALT="About Shelley"></A>
```

In the preceding lines of HTML we have added a NAME attribute to each of the six <IMG> tags. The name for each is the first word of the category that the graphic represents. Note that the first letter of each name is capitalized; JavaScript is case-sensitive. Now that we have the names of these images squared away we can move on to the creation of some new IMAGE objects that we will need for our script.

Because the images that we want to appear when the user rolls over one of the six graphics aren't explicitly placed on the page with HTML, we need to create two new IMAGE objects for each image we want to roll over. This will add these images to the images array and allow us to access their properties. Let's start by creating the IMAGE objects for the Products image.

```
<HEAD>
<SCRIPT Language="vJavaScript">
<!-- Code after this will be ignored by older browsers

      // Creation of the image objects
if (document.images)
{
ProductsOn=new Image(267, 64);
...
}
// Stop hiding the code here -->
</SCRIPT>
</HEAD>
```

In the preceding code we are initializing a new IMAGE object by using an image constructor with the following syntax:

```
New Image(width, height);
```

By putting the image constructor on the right-hand side of the assignment operator (=), and the name that we wish the IMAGE object to have on the left, we have just created a new IMAGE object called ProductsOn.

The naming of these new objects is very important to the operation of the script. The first part of the name should be the same as the name of the corresponding image that is already on the page. For example, in this first line where we are creating an object to hold the location of the rolled-over version of the Products graphic, the name starts with Products. Because this object holds the rolled-over version of the graphic, the second part of the name is On. When combined, we have a new object with the name ProductsOn. For each of the six navigation images, we are going to need not only an object to hold the rolled-over version of the graphic but one to hold a regular version of the graphic as well. This second object's name for our Products image will also start with Products but will end with Off. Let's add this new IMAGE object after our first one.

```
<HEAD>
<SCRIPT Language="JavaScript">
```

```
<!-- Code after this will be ignored by older browsers

     // Creation of the image objects
if (document.images)
{
ProductsOn=new Image(267, 64);
...
ProductsOff=new Image(267, 64);
...
}
// Stop hiding the code here -->
</SCRIPT>
</HEAD>
```

If you deviate from this naming convention, the functions that we are going to be writing won't know which IMAGE object to use for replacement and you will get errors. We now have the two new IMAGE objects that we will need for the Products rollover, but at the moment they are empty. Next, we need to assign actual images to them. We do this by assigning the location (URL) of the image to the source property of the IMAGE object, as follows:

```
<HEAD>
<SCRIPT Language="JavaScript ">
<!-- Code after this will be ignored by older browsers

if (document.images)
{
ProductsOn=new Image(267, 64);
ProductsOn.src="images/products_on.gif";

ProductsOff=new Image(267, 64);
ProductsOff.src="images/products_off.gif";
...
}
// Stop hiding the code here -->
</SCRIPT>
</HEAD>
```

We have completed On and Off objects for the Products rollover, but we also have to create objects for each of the other five image rollovers. We do this using the same naming conventions that we used for our first objects.

```
<HEAD>
<SCRIPT Language="JavaScript">
<!-- Code after this will be ignored by older browsers
```

```
if (document.images)
{
ProductsOn=new Image(267, 64);
ProductsOn.src="images/products_on.gif";

ProductsOff=new Image(267, 64);
ProductsOff.src="images/products_off.gif";


ServicesOn=new Image(267, 64);
ServicesOn.src="images/services_on.gif";

ServicesOff=new Image(267, 64);
ServicesOff.src="images/services_off.gif";


TrainingOn=new Image(267, 64);
TrainingOn.src="images/training_on.gif";

TrainingOff=new Image(267, 64);
TrainingOff.src="images/training_off.gif";


CommonOn=new Image(267, 64);
CommonOn.src="images/common_on.gif";

CommonOff=new Image(267, 64);
CommonOff.src="images/common_off.gif";


GeneticOn=new Image(267, 64);
GeneticOn.src="images/genetic_on.gif";

GeneticOff=new Image(267, 64);
GeneticOff.src="images/genetic_off.gif";


AboutOn=new Image(267, 64);
AboutOn.src="images/about_on.gif";

AboutOff=new Image(267, 64);
AboutOff.src="images/about_off.gif";
...
}
// Stop hiding the code here -->
</SCRIPT>
</HEAD>
```

Creating the IMAGE objects in this manner has another desired effect. When the browser creates the new IMAGE objects it loads the images into its cache, thereby preloading it into memory. This preloading allows the image to display immediately upon rollover. It is important to keep this preloading in mind when creating your HTML pages—if you do not put Height, Width, and alt attributes into your <IMG> tags, most browsers will not display the page until all of the content and images are loaded into memory. You can run into some serious load times if you have a lot of IMAGE objects loading for rollovers in the background, so make sure you put all of the necessary tags into your HTML.

We have successfully created IMAGE objects for all of the graphics that we need to accomplish our rollovers. Our next step is to create the functions that will run our rollovers.

Image Rollover Functions

When the user rolls over one of our graphics, JavaScript event handlers call the function we are going to write to actually perform the image replacements. Functions are an essential part of JavaScript; a function is a set of JavaScript statements that perform specific tasks. We will cover both defining and calling functions in this example, but for now, let's concentrate on defining the functions we need for our rollovers. You need four basic elements to define a function: the "function" keyword, a name for the function, a set of arguments that are separated with commas, and the statements that you want the function to execute.

We need to create two functions for our rollovers to work: one that switches to the "On" graphic when we roll over an image, and another to switch back to the "Off" graphic when we roll off the image. Generally, you will want to define the functions for a page in the head of your HTML, so let's start our functions right after our IMAGE objects.

```
function on(pic)
{
. . .
}
// Stop hiding the code here -->
</SCRIPT>
</HEAD>
```

The first step in defining a function is to call the `function` keyword followed by the name of the function; in this case, we'll call it `on`. Following the name, within a set of parentheses, we need to put a list of variables separated by commas—one for each argument we want to pass into the function. These variables will let us pass values into our function from the event handlers that call the function. We only need to pass a single argument into the function; we'll use the variable `pic` to hold that argument.

Next comes the set of instructions that we want the function to execute—these statements are enclosed within curly brackets.

```
function on(pic)
{
    if (document.images)
    {
        document.images[pic].src=eval(pic + "On.src");
    }
}
// Stop hiding the code here -->
</SCRIPT>
</HEAD>
```

The first statement that we want the function to execute is an `if` statement that will check for older browsers. If the browser supports the `IMAGE` object, the line following the `if` statement will be executed. In this line we are telling the browser to replace the source of the image that is being rolled over with the source of the `On` version of the graphic. A lot is happening in this line, so let's break it down into smaller parts. First, let's look at the left-hand side of the assignment operator (=).

```
document.images[pic].src
```

We are referencing the source property of the image located at the position in the `images` array that has the value of the variable `pic`—so let's say the value of `pic` is "Products." We are referencing the source property of the `Products IMAGE` object and assigning it the value passed to it from the right-hand side of the assignment operator.

If we had explicitly called the graphic product in the following manner:

```
document.product.src
```

we would need separate functions for every image that we wanted to give a rollover—not the most efficient way to code. When scripting, you should think about how you can most efficiently write your code. Any time you can use variables in this way it will save you a lot of time and trouble. There are, however, occasions when you will want to call a specific image each time the function is called, and the preceding line of code is an example of how to do that.

On the right-hand side of the operator we are going to use the `eval()` statement to combine the value of `pic` with a string to create a new value to assign as the source of the image being rolled over.

```
eval(pic + "On.src");
```

If the value of `pic` is "Products," the `eval()` statement will return `ProductsOn.src`, and the value of the source of the `ProductsOn` IMAGE object will be assigned to the source of the `Products` IMAGE object. When this happens, the image on the page will change to the On image until the user rolls off.

When the user rolls off the image, another function will be called. This is the second function that we have to create—let's call this function `off`.

```
function off(pic)
{
    if(document.images)
    {
        document.images[pic].src= eval(pic + "Off.src");
    }
}
// Stop hiding the code here -->
</SCRIPT>
</HEAD>
```

This function should look very similar to your On function; in fact, the only difference is that the second half of what is being evaluated on the right-hand side of the assignment operator is `Off.src` instead of `On.src`. Therefore, when this line is evaluated it will assign the source of the `ProductsOff` IMAGE object to be the source of the `Products` IMAGE object, thereby returning the image to its regular look.

Our functions are now complete and we are almost finished with the script. All that's left for us to do is to put the proper Java-Script event handlers into our HTML code.

Inserting the Event Handlers

You will find that most things in JavaScript are event driven. Events are generally the result of some action on the part of the user, such as rolling over a link or changing the value of a text field. To make use of these events with your JavaScript you must define an event handler to react to them. There are many predefined event handlers that you can use for this purpose; we will be using onMouseOver and onMouseOut for our rollovers. Let's first see what our existing HTML looks like without the event handlers.

```
<A HREF="products/index.html"><IMG SRC="images/
h_products_off.gif" WIDTH="71" HEIGHT="33" BORDER="0"
NAME="Products" ALT="Products"> </A>
```

For our purposes, we must add the event handlers to the ANCHOR tag. First, we add the onMouseOver handler.

```
<A HREF="products.html" onMouseOver="on('products');
return true;">
```

When an event handler is called it will execute any JavaScript statements that follow the handler. We enclose these statements in quotes and separate them with semicolons. The first thing we want our event handler to do is to call our on function. To call a function you simply call its name and enclose any values you wish to pass along to the function in parentheses separated by commas.

```
on('Products');
```

The preceding statement will call the on function and pass it the value Products; again, we are passing it Products because that is the name of the image that we want our function to affect.

Another common addition to rollovers is the displaying of a relevant phrase in the browser's status bar. To do this, we need to add another statement to our event handler.

```
<A HREF="products.html" onMouseOver="on('products');
window.status='Products'; return true;">
```

By calling on the WINDOW object's status property we are able to display any given text in the browser's status bar by assigning it a new value. The last addition that we need to make to our event handler is the following statement:

```
return true;
```

This statement tells the JavaScript engine that this is the end of what needs to be executed in the event handler and it can go on with the rest of its business.

Well, one event handler down, and one more to go. Let's add our `onMouseOut` handler to take care of things when the user rolls off an image.

```
<A HREF="products.html" onMouseOver="on('products');
window.status='Products'; return true; "
onMouseOut="off('products'); window.status=' '; return
true;">
```

For our `onMouseOut` handler we are calling the `off` function and again passing it the name of the graphic that we want to affect. To turn off the phrase that we put into the status bar, we now reset the `window.status` to a blank value and then leave the handler with the `return` statement.

Once we have inserted the event handlers for the `Products` image, we need to add some for the rest of the images. The syntax will be similar—just remember to change the value that you are passing to the functions to the name of the graphic that you want to be changed.

REVIEWING THE SCRIPT

We should now have all of the elements that we need to get our Web site up and running with some great rollovers. Let's take a look at the completed script and go over what we did in each section.

First, we created the `IMAGE` objects that we need in our script.

```
<SCRIPT Language="JavaScript">
<!-- Code after this will be ignored by older browsers

if (document.images)
{
ProductsOn=new Image(267, 64);
ProductsOn.src="images/products_on.gif";

ProductsOff=new Image(267, 64);
ProductsOff.src="images/products_off.gif";


ServicesOn=new Image(267, 64);
ServicesOn.src="images/services_on.gif";
```

```
ServicesOff=new Image(267, 64);
ServicesOff.src="images/services_off.gif";


TrainingOn=new Image(267, 64);
TrainingOn.src="images/training_on.gif";

TrainingOff=new Image(267, 64);
TrainingOff.src="images/training_off.gif";


CommonOn=new Image(267, 64);
CommonOn.src="images/common_on.gif";

CommonOff=new Image(267, 64);
CommonOff.src="images/common_off.gif";


GeneticOn=new Image(267, 64);
GeneticOn.src="images/genetic_on.gif";

GeneticOff=new Image(267, 64);
GeneticOff.src="images/genetic_off.gif";


AboutOn=new Image(267, 64);
AboutOn.src="images/about_on.gif";

AboutOff=new Image(267, 64);
AboutOff.src="images/about_off.gif";
}
```

Here are the steps we took to create the needed IMAGE objects:

1. We set up cloaking for browsers that do not support IMAGE objects.

2. We added the NAME attribute to the six images on which we want to put rollovers.

3. We created a set of two new IMAGE objects for each of the six images that will be affected by our rollover script.

4. We assigned each of the IMAGE object's source property the location of the proper image file.

Next, we created the functions that run our rollovers.

```
function on(pic)
{
```

```
    if (document.images)
    {
    document.images[pic].src=eval(pic + "On.src");
    }
}

function off(pic)
{
    if(document.images)
    {
    document.images[pic].src= eval(pic + "Off.src");
    }
}
// Stop hiding the code here -->
</SCRIPT>
</HEAD>
```

Here are the steps we took to create the rollover functions:

1. We created an on function that changes the image the user is currently over to the rolled-over version of that graphic.

2. We wrote an off function that changed the graphic back to its default state when the user rolled off it.

3. We made changes to the <A HREF>tags in the existing HTML.

```
<A HREF="products/index.html"
onMouseOver="on('products'); window.status='Products';
return true; "  onMouseOut="off('products');
window.status=' '; return true; ">

<A HREF="services/index.html"
onMouseOver="on('services'); window.status='Services';
return true; "  onMouseOut="off('services');
window.status=' '; return true; ">

<A HREF="training/index.html"
onMouseOver="on('training'); window.status='Training';
return true; "  onMouseOut="off('training');
window.status=' '; return true; ">

<A HREF="common/index.html" onMouseOver="on('common');
window.status='Common Good Projects'; return true; "
onMouseOut="off('common'); window.status=' '; return true; ">

<A HREF="genetic/index.html" onMouseOver="on('genetic');
window.status='Genetic'; return true; ""
onMouseOut="off('genetic'); window.status=' '; return
true; ">
```

```
<A HREF="about/index.html" onMouseOver="on('about');
window.status='About Us'; return true; "
onMouseOut="off('about'); window.status=' '; return
true; ">
```

Here are the steps we took to insert the event handlers into the HTML:

1. We added the onMouseOver event handlers to each of the six images' <A HREF> tags.

   Within that handler we called the on function, passing it the name of the graphic that we were rolling over; changed the status bar to display a new message; and added the return command to exit the handler.

2. We added the onMouseOut event handlers to each of the six images' <A HREF> tags.

   Within that handler we called the off function, passing it the name of the graphic that we were rolling over; reset the status bar to nothing; and added the return command to exit the handler.

We introduced several new aspects of JavaScript in this first script, including:

- A new method of cloaking that looks for browsers that support specific objects needed in your script.
- An introduction to arrays, specifically the images array.
- How to create new IMAGE objects and how to change their source property.
- How to create a function.
- The concept of event handlers and how to use two of them: onMouseOver and onMouseOut.
- How to change the message being displayed in the status bar of the browser window.

◆ Project II: Adding Advanced Functionality to Our Rollovers

The boss likes the new homepage rollovers so much that he wants to add rollovers to all of the secondary pages on the Shelley site (see Figure 2–3). It should be a fairly simple job considering that we can, for the most part, use the same script we wrote for the homepage. However, we will have to make a few changes for them to work properly on the secondary pages.

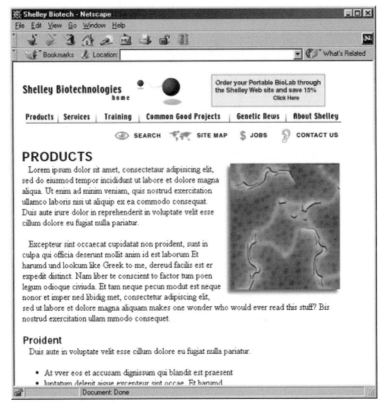

FIGURE 2–3 Shelley Biotech secondary page

First of all, we don't want the graphic for the section the user is currently in to be affected as a rollover; we want it to be the On version of the graphic at all times. This way, the user will always be able to tell which category he or she is in. To accomplish this we won't have to change our script; we simply take out the event handlers from that graphic's <A HREF> tag and change the image called in the <IMG> tag to the On version.

The other change we need to make is a little bit more complicated and requires us to modify the functions that we wrote for the homepage. What we want to do is to turn off the graphic for the category that we are in when we roll over any of the other navigation images. This will prevent two of the images from being in the On position at the same time, which might get confusing for the user. We are also going to have to make sure that once we roll off the images, the graphic for the section we are in goes back to the On position.

Inserting the Event Handlers

Before we get involved with the changes to the functions, let's first take care of the changes to the <A HREF> and <IMG> tags. Let's look at the section of HTML that contains the Products secondary page navigation images.

```
<A HREF="index.html"><IMG SRC="../images/
products_off.gif" WIDTH="71" HEIGHT="33" BORDER="0"
ALT="Products"></A>

<A HREF="../services/index.html"><IMG SRC="../images/
services_off.gif" WIDTH="67" HEIGHT="33" BORDER="0"
ALT="Services"></A>

<A HREF="../training/index.html"><IMG SRC="../images/
training_off.gif" WIDTH="75" HEIGHT="33" BORDER="0"
ALT="Training"></A>

<A HREF="../common/index.html"><IMG SRC="../images/
common_off.gif" WIDTH="157" HEIGHT="33" BORDER="0"
ALT="Common Good"></A>

<A HREF="../genetic/index.html"><IMG SRC="../images/
news_off.gif" WIDTH="98" HEIGHT="33" BORDER="0"
ALT="Genetic News"></A>

<A HREF="../about/index.html"><IMG SRC="../images/
about_off.gif" WIDTH="106" HEIGHT="33" BORDER="0"
ALT="About Shelley"></A></TD>
```

First, we need to change the image we are calling for the Products graphic to the On version (products_on.gif).

```
<IMG SRC="../images/products_on.gif" WIDTH="71"
HEIGHT="33" BORDER="0" ALT="Products">
```

Then, whenever the user is in the Products section, the Products navigation image will constantly be on. Next, we need to add the NAME attribute to <IMG> tags and insert the event handlers into the image's <A HREF> tags. When the user comes to this page the Products image will always be on, so we don't need to have that image participate in the rollovers. Therefore, we don't need to put event handlers in its <A HREF> tag.

```
<A HREF="index.html"><IMG SRC="../images/
products_on.gif" WIDTH="71" HEIGHT="33" BORDER="0"
NAME="Products" ALT="Products"></A>

<A HREF="../services/index.html"
onMouseOver="on('Services'); window.status='Services';
return true;" onMouseOut="off('Services');
window.status=' '; return true;"><IMG SRC="../images/
services_off.gif" WIDTH="67" HEIGHT="33" BORDER="0"
NAME="Services" ALT="Services"></A>

<A HREF="../training/index.html"
onMouseOver="on('Training'); window.status='Training';
return true;" onMouseOut="off('Training');
window.status=' '; return true;"><IMG SRC="../images/
training_off.gif" WIDTH="75" HEIGHT="33" BORDER="0"
NAME="Training" ALT="Training"></A>

<A HREF="../common/index.html"
onMouseOver="on('Common'); window.status='Common Good
Projects'; return true;" onMouseOut="off('Common');
window.status=' '; return true;"><IMG SRC="../images/
common_off.gif" WIDTH="157" HEIGHT="33" BORDER="0"
NAME="Common" ALT="Common Good"></A>

<A HREF="../genetic/index.html" onMouseOver="on('News');
window.status='Genetic News'; return true;"
onMouseOut="off('News'); window.status=' '; return
true;"><IMG SRC="../images/news_off.gif" WIDTH="98"
HEIGHT="33" BORDER="0" NAME="News" ALT="Genetic News"></A>

<A HREF="../about/index.html" onMouseOver="on('About');
window.status='About Us'; return true;"
onMouseOut="off('About'); window.status=' '; return
true;"><IMG SRC="../images/about_off.gif" WIDTH="106"
HEIGHT="33" BORDER="0" NAME="About" ALT="About Shelley"></A>
</TD>
```

The event handlers should look very familiar because they are the same ones that we inserted in our homepage rollover script. Finding ways to reuse code that you have already written is a great way to save time and enhance your efficiency. The NAME attribute has also been added to all of the <IMG> tags; notice that even though we didn't insert event handlers for the Products image, we still put in the NAME attribute. The reason for this will become clear later in our script. Our next step is to create IMAGE objects for all of our rollover images.

Creating the IMAGE Objects

This is another area in which we will have some luck: The IMAGE objects that we created for the homepage will work very nicely for all of our secondary pages with just slight modifications. The only thing we have to change is the path that we are assigning to the source property of the object. Because the secondary pages exist in directories that are one level deeper than the homepage, we will need to tell the object to go back up one level before it looks to the Images directory.

First, let's copy the existing IMAGE objects from the homepage into the "Products" page and then we'll make the necessary changes.

```
<SCRIPT Language="JavaScript">
<!-- Code after this will be ignored by older browsers

// Creating Image Objects for Rollovers
if (document.images)
{
ProductsOn=new Image(71, 33);
ProductsOn.src="images/products_on.gif";

ProductsOff=new Image(71, 33);
ProductsOff.src="images/products_off.gif";


ServicesOn=new Image(67, 33);
ServicesOn.src="images/services_on.gif";

ServicesOff=new Image(67, 33);
ServicesOff.src="images/services_off.gif";


TrainingOn=new Image(75, 33);
TrainingOn.src="images/training_on.gif";

TrainingOff=new Image(75, 33);
TrainingOff.src="images/training_off.gif";


CommonOn=new Image(157, 33);
CommonOn.src="images/common_on.gif";
```

```
CommonOff=new Image(157, 33);
CommonOff.src="images/common_off.gif";


NewsOn=new Image(98, 33);
NewsOn.src="images/news_on.gif";

NewsOff=new Image(98, 33);
NewsOff.src="images/news_off.gif";


AboutOn=new Image(106, 33);
AboutOn.src="images/about_on.gif";

AboutOff=new Image(106, 33);
AboutOff.src="images/about_off.gif";
}
...

// Stop hiding the code here -->
</SCRIPT>
</HEAD>
```

Now we need to go in and modify the path for the source property of the objects.

```
<SCRIPT Language="JavaScript">
<!-- Code after this will be ignored by older browsers

// Creating Image Objects for Rollovers
if (document.images)
{
ProductsOn=new Image(71, 33);
ProductsOn.src="../images/products_on.gif";

ProductsOff=new Image(71, 33);
ProductsOff.src="../images/products_off.gif";


ServicesOn=new Image(67, 33);
ServicesOn.src="../images/services_on.gif";

ServicesOff=new Image(67, 33);
ServicesOff.src="../images/services_off.gif";


TrainingOn=new Image(75, 33);
TrainingOn.src="../images/training_on.gif";
```

```
TrainingOff=new Image(75, 33);
TrainingOff.src="../images/training_off.gif";


CommonOn=new Image(157, 33);
CommonOn.src="../images/common_on.gif";

CommonOff=new Image(157, 33);
CommonOff.src="../images/common_off.gif";


NewsOn=new Image(98, 33);
NewsOn.src="../images/news_on.gif";

NewsOff=new Image(98, 33);
NewsOff.src="../images/news_off.gif";


AboutOn=new Image(106, 33);
AboutOn.src="../images/about_on.gif";

AboutOff=new Image(106, 33);
AboutOff.src="../images/about_off.gif";
}
...

// Stop hiding the code here -->
</SCRIPT>
</HEAD>
```

The last step is to put in our rollover functions and make the changes needed for them to work on the secondary pages.

Inserting the Rollover Functions

We can start by just copying the functions that we used on the homepage. As stated earlier, they will need to be modified to work on the secondary pages; but since the core functionality is the same, we won't have to start the functions from scratch.

```
// Image Rollover Functions
function on(pic)
{
    if (document.images)
    {
        document.images[pic].src=eval(pic + "On.src");
    }
}
```

```
function off(pic)
{
     if(document.images)
     {
          document.images[pic].src= eval(pic + "Off.src");
     }
}
```

We have our basic functions in the page now, so let's take a closer look at the problem that we have to solve in order for them to work properly. On the secondary pages, we have changed the HTML so that the navigation graphic for whichever section we are currently in is in the On position. Therefore, when the user rolls over one of the other categories, both that graphic and the graphic for the section that the user is currently in will be highlighted. This could lead to some confusion on the part of the user, so what we need to do is turn off the graphic of the section we are currently in while the user rolls over one of the other categories.

To do this we are going to have to make slight modifications to both the on and the off functions, as well as create a new function, off1, that will handle some of the extra functionality we are going to need. Let's start with modifications to the on function.

```
// Image Rollover Functions

...

function on (pic)
{
     if   (document.images)
     {
     document.images[pic].src=eval (pic + "On.src");
     document.images['Products'].src=eval
     ("ProductsOff.src");
          ...
     }
}
...
```

The line we added in the script tells the JavaScript runtime engine to turn off the graphic for the Products section after turning on the graphic the user has rolled over. Note that we have specifically called the Products image by name and have explicitly referenced the object source that we want to assign to it. Therefore, we need to change this line for each of the sections on the site so the script will turn off the proper image.

We now have the image of the section we are in turning off when the user rolls over another image. Next, we need a way to turn it back on when the user rolls off the image. The simplest way to accomplish this is to put a line of code in the off function that just turns the graphic of the section we are in to the On position when it is called. Unfortunately, this method has a flaw: If the user were to quickly roll over the category images one after another, the image for the category the user is in would flicker on and off. This isn't the end of the world, but it's kind of tacky and requires a more complex solution.

What we need is a way to tell not only if the user has rolled off an image, but whether or not the user has rolled over one of the other images before we turn the selected category image back on. The first step is to create a variable in which we can store a value and use it to test whether or not the user has rolled over an image.

```
// Image Rollover Functions

var over_checker;

function on (pic)
{
     if   (document.images)
     {
     document.images[pic].src=eval (pic + "On.src");
     document.images['Products'].src=eval
     ("ProductsOff.src");
          . . .
     }
}
. . .
```

In the preceding code, we declared the over_checker variable at the beginning of our rollover functions. The first place we need to use this is in our on function, because we need to know if the user is currently rolling over a category image. We set over_checker to hold the value of "on" when the on function is called.

```
// Image Rollover Functions

var over_checker;

function on (pic)
{
     if   (document.images)
     {
     document.images[pic].src=eval (pic + "On.src");
```

```
document.images['Products'].src=eval
("ProductsOff.src");

over_checker='on';
}
}
...
```

Not only do we need to know when the user has rolled over an image, but we also need to know when the user has rolled off an image. To accomplish this we need to modify our off function.

```
function off (pic)
{
    if (document.images)
    {
    over_checker='off';
    document.images[pic].src=eval (pic + "Off.src");
        ...
    }
}
...
```

Just like our on function we added a line that assigns a value to our over_checker variable; in this case, we are assigning it the value off. This will let us know when the user has rolled off an image.

Well, knowing if the user is over a graphic is all well and good, but how are we going to use that information? Enter our third function. This function will look at our over_checker variable and, if nothing is rolled over, then it will turn the graphic for the section that the user is in back to the On position. Let's take a look at our new function:

```
function off1 ()
{
    if (over_checker=='off')
    {
    if (document.images)
        {
        document.images['Products'].src=eval
        ("ProductsOn.src");
        }
    }
}
```

Several things are happening in this new function, but there are no new concepts that we haven't already covered. Even so, let's go through it and see just what is going on. First, we are using an `if` statement to check and see if the value of `over_checker` is `off`. If this is the case, then the script moves down and checks to see if the user's browser supports image rollovers. If it does, the script then turns on the graphic of the section the user is in. As in the line of code added to our `on` function, we are explicitly calling for the `Products` image to be turned back on. Once we finish the code for the rest of the secondary sections, we will need to change the image being affected.

There is one final piece of code that is missing from our functions. Currently, our new `off1` function is never called. The logical place to put the call is in our `off` function, so that when the user rolls off an image the `off1` function will be called; and if the user hasn't rolled over another image, then the chosen category's graphic will change. There is, however, an issue with just putting in a normal call to the function: Since the JavaScript engine interprets the code so quickly, the user could not possibly roll over another image quickly enough to prevent the function from turning on the graphic for the section. Therefore, we need to set a delay so that the `off1` function will be called after a brief pause, allowing the user to roll over a new image.

To accomplish this we will use a new method: `setTimeout()`. This method executes its arguments after a user-defined amount of time. Let's take a quick look at its syntax.

```
setTimeout(arguments, msec)
```

For our purposes, we only need to give it one argument—a call to our `off1` function. Only a short pause is needed to give the user the time he or she needs to roll over a new image; in this case, 700 milliseconds will do the trick. Let's look at the new line of code once we add it to our `off` function.

```
function off (pic)
{
      if (document.images)
      {
      over_checker='off';
      document.images[pic].src=eval (pic + "Off.src");
      setTimeout ("off1()", 700);
```

```
        }
    }
```

The last piece of code we added tells the JavaScript runtime engine to call the function `off1` after 700 milliseconds, which will then take care of the rest of the work for us. We are now finished adding our enhanced rollovers to the `Products` section of the site.

REVIEWING THE SCRIPT

While most of our script for this project was repurposed from our rollovers on the homepage, we made some changes and added some new functionality to our rollovers. Let's review exactly what we did for this project.

First, we inserted the necessary event handlers and made the changes to the `<IMG>` tags.

```
<A HREF="index.html"><IMG SRC="../images/
products_on.gif" WIDTH="71" HEIGHT="33" BORDER="0"
NAME="Products" ALT="Products"></A>

<A HREF="../services/index.html"
onMouseOver="on('Services'); window.status='Services';
return true;" onMouseOut="off('Services');
window.status=' '; return true;"><IMG SRC="../images/
services_off.gif" WIDTH="67" HEIGHT="33" BORDER="0"
NAME="Services" ALT="Services"></A>

<A HREF="../training/index.html"
onMouseOver="on('Training'); window.status='Training';
return true;" onMouseOut="off('Training');
window.status=' '; return true;"><IMG SRC="../images/
training_off.gif" WIDTH="75" HEIGHT="33" BORDER="0"
NAME="Training" ALT="Training"></A>

<A HREF="../common/index.html"
onMouseOver="on('Common'); window.status='Common Good
Projects'; return true;" onMouseOut="off('Common');
window.status=' '; return true;"><IMG SRC="../images/
common_off.gif" WIDTH="157" HEIGHT="33" BORDER="0"
NAME="Common" ALT="Common Good"></A>

<A HREF="../genetic/index.html" onMouseOver="on('News');
window.status='Genetic News'; return true;"
onMouseOut="off('News'); window.status=' '; return
true;"><IMG SRC="../images/news_off.gif" WIDTH="98"
HEIGHT="33" BORDER="0" NAME="News" ALT="Genetic News"></A>
```

```
<A HREF="../about/index.html" onMouseOver="on('About');
window.status='About Us'; return true;"
onMouseOut="off('About'); window.status=' '; return
true;"><IMG SRC="../images/about_off.gif" WIDTH="106"
HEIGHT="33" BORDER="0" NAME="About" ALT="About Shelley"></A>
</TD>
```

Let's look at the steps we took in this part of our script:

1. We added the onMouseOver event handlers to the <A HREF> tags of all the images, except for the Products image.

   Within that handler we called the on function, passing it the name of the graphic that we were rolling over; changed the status bar to display a new message; and added the return command to exit the handler.

2. We added the onMouseOut event handlers to the <A HREF> tags of all the images, except for the Products image.

   Within that handler we called the off function, passing it the name of the graphic that we were rolling over; reset the status bar to nothing; and added the return command to exit the handler.

3. We inserted the NAME attribute into all six <IMG> tags.

   Even though we didn't put event handlers into the <A HREF> tag of the Products image, we still needed to give it a NAME attribute because we will be changing its state when the user rolls over one of the other five images.

After inserting the event handlers and NAME attributes, we created the IMAGE objects we need in our rollover script.

```
<SCRIPT Language="JavaScript">
<!-- Code after this will be ignored by older browsers

// Creating Image Objects for Rollovers
if (document.images)
{
ProductsOn=new Image(71, 33);
ProductsOn.src="../images/products_on.gif";

ProductsOff=new Image(71, 33);
ProductsOff.src="../images/products_off.gif";


ServicesOn=new Image(67, 33);
ServicesOn.src="../images/services_on.gif";
```

```
ServicesOff=new Image(67, 33);
ServicesOff.src="../images/services_off.gif";


TrainingOn=new Image(75, 33);
TrainingOn.src="../images/training_on.gif";

TrainingOff=new Image(75, 33);
TrainingOff.src="../images/training_off.gif";


CommonOn=new Image(157, 33);
CommonOn.src="../images/common_on.gif";

CommonOff=new Image(157, 33);
CommonOff.src="../images/common_off.gif";


NewsOn=new Image(98, 33);
NewsOn.src="../images/news_on.gif";

NewsOff=new Image(98, 33);
NewsOff.src="../images/news_off.gif";


AboutOn=new Image(106, 33);
AboutOn.src="../images/about_on.gif";

AboutOff=new Image(106, 33);
AboutOff.src="../images/about_off.gif";
}
```

Here are the steps we took to create the IMAGE objects:

1. We copied the IMAGE objects that we had created for the homepage rollovers.

2. We then pointed the source property of the objects toward the correct path.

3. We put in the functions that power the script.

```
// Image Rollover Functions

var over_checker;

function on (pic)
{
     if  (document.images)
     {
```

```
document.images[pic].src=eval (pic + "On.src");
document.images['Products'].src=eval
("ProductsOff.src");

over_checker='on';
}
}

function off (pic)
{
    if (document.images)
    {
    over_checker='off';
    document.images[pic].src=eval (pic + "Off.src");
    setTimeout ("off1('Products')", 700);
    }
}

function off1 ()
{
    if (over_checker=='off')
    {
        if (document.images)
        {
        document.images['Products'].src=eval
        ("ProductsOn.src");
        }
    }
}
// Stop hiding the code here -->
</SCRIPT>
</HEAD>
```

Here are the steps we followed to create the functions:

1. We copied the on and off functions from our rollover script on the homepage, and used them as the basis for our modified on and off functions.

2. We modified our on function:

   We created the variable over_checker at the beginning of our rollover functions.

   Within the on function we assigned the value "on" to the variable over_checker.

   We added a line to turn the Products image to the off position.

3. We modified the off function:

We added a line that assigns the value "off" to the variable over_checker.

We put in the setTimeout method, which will call the off1 function after a delay of 700 milliseconds.

4. We created the off1 function.

This function runs two tests using if statements: First, it checks that the value of over_checker is set to "off," and then it checks that the user's browser supports rollovers.

If both of these tests return a value of true, then the function sets the Products image to the on position.

We have been introduced to some new aspects of JavaScript in this script:

- The setTimeout method.
- The concept of repurposing older scripts for new uses.

◆ Rollover Quirks

Rollovers can be a very useful and exciting addition to your Web site; however, there are some quirks that you should keep in mind when using them. First, not everyone is going to be able to see your rollovers—anyone using a version of Netscape older than 3.0 or Internet Explorer 3.0 won't be able to see them. While this surely isn't a big enough deterrent to dissuade you from using rollovers, you should keep it in mind. It's not a good idea to have navigation that is only accessible through the use of a rollover; it's always good etiquette to include at least back-up text navigation for those with older browsers.

The following quirk rears its head in Netscape 3.0: When using images inside nested tables, if you have a table that is nested into another table, and an image is located in that nested table, the Java-Script engine will create two array entries for that single graphic. If the image were in a table that was nested inside two tables, then three entries would be created in the images array. This can lead to problems if you are referring to your images based on their location in the IMAGE array instead of by name.

A final anomaly that you should keep an eye out for is found when using animated gifs in your rollovers. If you are using the same animated image for multiple rollovers and a single IMAGE object, you will find that the animation will only work on the first rollover. On all subsequent rollovers it will skip to the last frame of the animation.

The workaround for this is to make separate IMAGE objects for every instance where you want the animated gif to show up on a rollover.

RECAP

You will find that image rollovers are by far the most commonly used JavaScript being implemented on Web sites today. Almost every site you visit makes use of them in one way or another, so a good knowledge of how they work and what their limitations are can be a great asset to a programmer. Once you have the basics down, use that knowledge to experiment with different rollover techniques. You will be surprised at some of the creative and exciting rollovers you can devise.

ADVANCED PROJECTS

1. Create a homepage on which multiple graphics change when one of the main category graphics is rolled over.

2. Create a page on which a random image replaces an existing image when the category images are rolled over.

3 JavaScript for Navigation

IN THIS CHAPTER

- Project I: JavaScript and Pull-Down Menus
- Project II: Using Multiple Pull-Down Menus for Navigation
- Project III: Using JavaScript on a Log-in Page
- Recap
- Advanced Projects

So far you have done a great job adding some new functionality and pizzazz to Shelley Biotech's homepage. Now that your boss has seen how great Java-Script can be, another idea has popped into his head. The powers that be would love to be able to add a pull-down menu to the homepage and allow the user to jump quickly to certain pages that are several levels down in the site with only a single click. Of course, like most of your projects, they need it done ASAP, so it's off we go on another assignment.

After meeting with one of the designers, you feel that you have worked out a good place to put the pull-down menu on the homepage (see Figure 3–1). Now you just need to get the links for the pull-down menu. An e-mail to your boss takes care of that easily enough and you're soon ready to go.

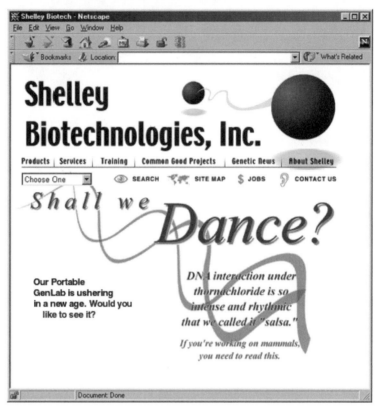

FIGURE 3–1 Pull-down menu added to the homepage

◆ Project I: JavaScript and Pull-Down Menus

The first thing we need to do to the homepage is insert the HTML code that will give us our pull-down menu and Go button. Here is the code that we will be using:

```
<SELECT NAME="PullDown">
     <OPTION VALUE="default">Get There Quick
     <OPTION VALUE="whatsnew.html">What's New
     <OPTION VALUE="products/featured.html">Feature Product
     <OPTION VALUE="news/press.html">Press Releases
     <OPTION VALUE="store/index.html">Company Store
</SELECT>

<INPUT TYPE="Button" NAME="Go" VALUE="Go">
```

Because we will be inserting the pull-down into a preexisting design, we are going to place the <FORM> tags at the beginning and end of the HTML body instead of directly around the form element to prevent any unwanted line breaks or spaces. You will also notice that the value properties of the options are left blank; we will be filling those in later when we insert the event handler needed to run the script.

Creating the Navigation Function

Since the navigation pull-down menu is going to be on a page that already has image rollovers, we can insert our function within the existing <SCRIPT> tags. We will insert our new function directly after the image rollover functions as follows:

```
function off(pic)

{
      if(document.images)
      {
      document.images[pic].src= eval(pic + "Off.src");
      }
}

// Pull-Down Menu Navigation Function

function PageChanger(page)
{
      . . .
}
```

The function itself will be fairly simple and will consist of two parts. You will notice that we will pass a value into the function that gets assigned to the variable page. This value will be the location of the page that the user has selected from the pull-down menu. In the first line we are going to use that value to change the location property of the DOCUMENT object; this will reload the browser window with the new Web page.

```
// Pull-Down Menu Navigation Function

function PageChanger(page)
{
      document.location= page;
      . . .
}
```

Next, we will add a line that serves a housekeeping function more than anything else. When the function is run, this line will reset the pull-down menu to the first choice in the menu. This isn't too helpful in our case because the page is changing; however, it is a nice little touch if the pull-down menu were changing the location of another frame instead of the whole window.

```
// Pull-Down Menu Navigation Function

function PageChanger(page)
{
    document.location= page;
    document.NavForm.PullDown.options[0].selected=true;
}
```

Inserting the Event Handler

Now that we have created our function, we need to insert the event handler into our HTML to call the function. Before we do that, let's insert the value properties into the pull-down menu's options. As stated earlier, the value that we are passing into our function is the URL for the page we want to send the user to. This value comes from the VALUE attribute of our menu options. Therefore, for the value of each option, we need to put the location of the page for that selection.

```
<SELECT NAME="PullDown">
    <OPTION VALUE=" ">Get There Quick
    <OPTION VALUE="whatsnew.html">What's New
    <OPTION VALUE="products/featured.html">Feature Product
    <OPTION VALUE="news/press.html">Press Releases
    <OPTION VALUE="store/index.html">Company Store
</SELECT>
```

For the first menu option, which is just a title inserted for aesthetic purposes, we don't put in a value because we don't want that option to send the user anywhere. Once the user selects the desired menu option, he or she needs to click on the Go button to get to the new page. To accomplish this we will insert the onClick handler into the HTML for the Go button.

```
<SELECT NAME="PullDown">
    <OPTION VALUE=" ">Get There Quick
    <OPTION VALUE="whatsnew.html">What's New
    <OPTION VALUE="products/featured.html">Feature Product
    <OPTION VALUE="news/press.html">Press Releases
```

```
        <OPTION VALUE="store/index.html">Company Store
</SELECT>

<INPUT TYPE="Button" NAME="Go" VALUE=Go"
onClick="PageChanger(document.NavForm.PullDown
.options[NavForm.PullDown.selectedIndex].value)">
```

We are performing two actions in the event handler: We are calling the `PageChanger()` function and we are passing a value to it. The value that we are passing is the value of the option that the user has chosen from the pull-down menu. In the functions we have created so far, the value that we have passed into the function has been a simple string. In this event handler, we are trying something new: We are referencing the pull-down menu object and accessing the value that is currently selected. This value is then passed into the function and used to send the user to the page he or she wants to visit.

Our script is now functional and ready to go. However, because of the Go button we added to the page, the categories to the right of the pull-down menu now take up two lines (see Figure 3–2). Unfortunately, this is unacceptable, so we need to find another solution. Luckily, there is another way we can power our script that will not only take care of this problem, but will make navigating with the pull-down menu even faster.

Using onChange for Instant Gratification

To get the page layout back to its original state we need to get rid of the Go button; however, at the moment, it contains the event handler that is running our script. What we need is a handler that we can put into the pull-down menu itself that will run our script for us—the `onChange` event handler. This handler looks for a change in the state of the object in which it is contained, and when it finds one, it triggers.

Once we insert it in our pull-down menu, we can have it activate our function when the user changes the menu option from the default option that is loaded with the page. Let's see how this changes our HTML code.

```
<SELECT NAME="PullDown"
onChange="PageChanger(this.options[this.selectedIndex]
.value)">
        <OPTION VALUE=" ">Get There Quick
        <OPTION VALUE="whatsnew.html">What's New
        <OPTION VALUE="products/featured.html">Feature Product
```

FIGURE 3–2 Page with pull-down menu and Go button

```
        <OPTION VALUE="news/press.html">Press Releases
        <OPTION VALUE="store/index.html">Company Store
</SELECT>
```

First, you will notice that we have removed the Go button because it is no longer needed. Second, the onChange event handler has been added to the pull-down menu. The value we are passing to the function is the same—it's the value of the option the user has selected. However, we are calling that value differently than the way we called it before. Because the event handler is in the form element from which we wish to get the value, we can use the following method:

```
this.options[this.selectedIndex].value
```

This line of code in the script tells the JavaScript runtime engine to get the information from the form element that contains the event handler. Both methods work equally well, and it's always good to be exposed to multiple ways of accomplishing a task.

With the insertion of the new event handler, our script is finished and ready to work. By using the onChange handler, the page now changes as soon as the user makes a choice from the menu, without having to press a button.

REVIEWING THE SCRIPT

Let's look at what we did to create this script. First, we created a function that will accept a value from a form element and use it to send the user to another HTML page. We also went over two different event handlers that can be used to drive the scripts.

First, let's look at the function:

```
// Pull-Down Menu Navigation Function

 function PageChanger(page)
 {
     document.location= page;
     document.NavForm.PullDown.options[0].selected=true;
 }

</SCRIPT>
```

1. We created the function PageChanger().

The first thing we did in the function was to set the location property of the DOCUMENT object to the value contained within the variable page. This value is the URL that is being passed into the function from the pull-down menu.

Next, we reset the option that appears in the pull-down menu to the first option.

Next, let's look at the HTML needed for use with the onClick handler.

```
<SELECT NAME="PullDown">
     <OPTION VALUE=" ">Get There Quick
     <OPTION VALUE="whatsnew.html">What's New
     <OPTION VALUE="products/featured.html">Feature Product
     <OPTION VALUE="news/press.html">Press Releases
     <OPTION VALUE="store/index.html">Company Store
</SELECT>
```

```
<INPUT TYPE="Button" NAME="Go" VALUE="Go"
onClick="PageChanger(document.NavForm.PullDown
.options[NavForm.PullDown.selectedIndex].value)">
```

2. Our function will be called when the user clicks on the
   Go button. We inserted the `onClick` event handler into
   the button form element.

   Within the event handler, we are calling our `PageChanger()`
   function and passing it the value held by the menu option
   that has been chosen from the pull-down menu.

Once it was decided that we would have to take the Go button
off the page because of design issues, we opted to use the `onChange`
event handler.

```
<SELECT NAME="PullDown"
onChange="PageChanger(this.options[this.selectedIndex]
.value)">
    <OPTION VALUE=" ">Get There Quick
    <OPTION VALUE="whatsnew.html">What's New
    <OPTION VALUE="products/featured.html">Feature Product
    <OPTION VALUE="news/press.html">Press Releases
    <OPTION VALUE="store/index.html">Company Store
</SELECT>
```

3. We inserted the `onChange` event handler into our pull-
   down menu.

   Again, within this event handler, we are calling our
   `PageChanger()` function and passing it the URL of the
   selected menu option.

Let's take a look at the new concepts that we have covered
during this project:

- Accessing and changing the location property of the DOC-
  UMENT object.
- Accessing the values of pull-down menu options and
  changing the option that is selected within a pull-down
  menu.
- The `onClick` and `onChange` event handlers.

As Web sites become more and more important to the success
of companies, the content that they hold grows by leaps and
bounds. Finding quick and efficient methods to navigate the

information is now more important than ever. Using the `onClick` and `onChange` event handlers along with a pull-down menu is a good way to get people the information they need.

◆ Project II: Using Multiple Pull-Down Menus for Navigation

With the success of our pull-down navigation script, the boss has thought of another area of the company's Web site that could benefit from pull-down menu navigation—the Company Store section. At the moment, navigating the various product groups and products is cumbersome and not very intuitive for the user. Shelley Biotech is about to launch a new wave of products, and this would be a perfect opportunity to give the section a facelift (see Figure 3–3). It would be great if we could use pull-down menus and JavaScript to increase efficiency and usability.

The boss wants to have two pull-down menus—one that contains a list of the different product groups, and another that dynamically populates itself with the products of the group that is chosen from the first pull-down menu. The user would then be sent to the page that corresponds with any product chosen from the second menu.

This may sound like a daunting task at the moment, but we have already learned much of what we will need to accomplish it in the previous chapters. This project will be broken into four sections: creating the arrays that will hold the product information needed for each of the product groups; creating the function that dynamically populates the second menu; creating the function that will handle navigation; and inserting the proper event handlers into the HTML code.

Creating the Arrays

With all the new products that are coming out, the marketing department is not sure which product groups and products they want to include in the navigation. They do know, however, that there will be at least four product groups containing a minimum of five products each. Using this information, we will create a navigation menu system using placeholders that can be replaced by the real product data at a later date. With that said, let's get started.

We already had a brief introduction to the concept of arrays in the first two chapters. We have learned how to access the arrays that

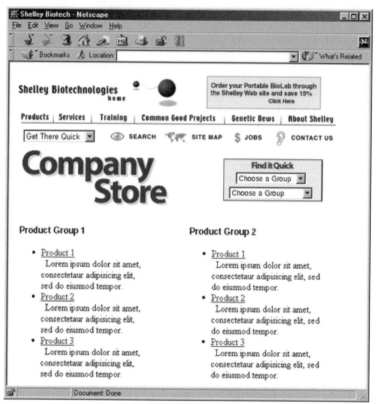

FIGURE 3–3 The Company Store section of the Shelley Web site

are created by the JavaScript engine as a page is loaded and how to add objects to some of those arrays. Now, however, we need to create some arrays of our own and populate them with the updated product information to complete the job.

To create an array you use the following syntax:

```
arrayObjectName = new Array([arrayLength])
```

In the preceding statement, `arrayObjectName` is a place-holder for the name you wish to give the array, and `array-Length` is a placeholder for the number of entries in your array.

We will need two values for each product in order to dynamically insert a choice for it in the second pull-down menu: The first is the product's name and the second is the location of the HTML page to which it corresponds. To store this data we will create two arrays for each product group—one that stores the product names and another that holds the locations of the pages. Since we don't know the names of the product groups, we will use group1, group2, group3, and group4 to identify them. As in the first project, we will add our new code to the existing <SCRIPT> tag after the code, which already appears on the page.

```
// Arrays for Products

    //Define the arrays

group1_names = new Array(5);
group1_locations = new Array(5);

group2_names = new Array(5);
group2_locations = new Array(5);

group3_names = new Array(5);
group3_locations = new Array(5);

group4_names = new Array(5);
group4_locations = new Array(5);


    ...
```

Let's look at the code that defines the first set of arrays:

```
group1_names = new Array(5);
group1_locations = new Array(5);
```

The first line defines a new array, group1_names, and assigns it a length of 5, which is the number of products that we were told we could expect for each group—this array will hold the names of the products from group1. The second line defines a new array, group1_locations, and assigns it a length of 5 as well—this array will hold the locations of the pages for the products in group1. After defining the arrays for product group1, we then created the arrays for the other three groups.

Now that the arrays have been defined, we need to populate them with information about the products. First, let's take a quick look at the syntax for adding an entry to an array:

```
arrayName[arrayPosition] = "arrayValue"
```

arrayName is the name of the array to which you wish to add an entry; arrayPosition is the position in the array in which you want to store the value; and `arrayValue` is the actual value that you wish to store in the array.

Let's populate `group1`'s arrays with its product information:

```
// Populate Group1's Arrays

group1_names[0] = 'Group1_product one';
group1_locations[0] = 'group1/prod_1.html';

group1_names[1] = 'Group1_product two';
group1_locations[1] = 'group1/prod_2.html';

group1_names[2] = 'Group1_product three';
group1_locations[2] = 'group1/prod_3.html';

group1_names[3] = 'Group1_product four';
group1_locations[3] = 'group1/prod_4.html';

group1_names[4] = 'Group1_product five';
group1_locations[4] = 'group1/prod_5.html';

var group1_length = group1_names.length;
```

In the preceding code, we assigned a product name and a product page location to the two different arrays at the same position in each array. In other words, after these first two lines:

```
group1_names[0] = 'Group1_product one';
group1_locations[0] = 'group1/prod_1.html';
```

we have assigned the value product one to the first position in the `group1_names` array, and the value `group1/prod_1.html` to the first position in the `group1_locations` array. The rest of this code puts the information for the remaining products into the two arrays at positions corresponding to their numbers. As with the naming of the groups, we are using placeholders for the product names and their page locations.

There will be many times when you are working on a project and you may not have the finalized content for your pages. Using placeholder content allows you to finish your coding so that when you receive the finalized content, all you have to do is drop it in. The trick is to use placeholder values that are clear and easily decipherable, just in case you are not the person inserting the final content.

The last line in our code for populating the `group1` arrays is as follows:

```
var group1_length = group1_names.length;
```

This line assigns the length of the `group1` arrays to the variable `group1_length`; we do this by accessing the `length` property of the `ARRAY` object. We will use this variable later in the function that will populate the second menu.

Here is the rest of the code that will populate the arrays for the other product groups. It shares the same structure as that of the first group:

```
// Populate Group2's Arrays

group2_names[0] = 'Group2_product one';
group2_locations[0] = 'group2/prod_1.html';

group2_names[1] = 'Group2_product two';
group2_locations[1] = 'group2/prod_2.html';

group2_names[2] = 'Group2_product three';
group2_locations[2] = 'group2/prod_3.html';

group2_names[3] = 'Group2_product four';
group2_locations[3] = 'group2/prod_4.html';

group2_names[4] = 'Group2_product five';
group2_locations[4] = 'group2/prod_5.html';

var group2_length = group2_names.length;


// Populate Group3's Arrays

group3_names[0] = 'Group3_product one';
group3_locations[0] = 'group3/prod_1.html';

group3_names[1] = 'Group3_product two';
group3_locations[1] = 'group3/prod_2.html';

group3_names[2] = 'Group3_product three';
group3_locations[2] = 'group3/prod_3.html';

group3_names[3] = 'Group3_product four';
group3_locations[3] = 'group3/prod_4.html';

group3_names[4] = 'Group3_product five';
group3_locations[4] = 'group3/prod_5.html';

var group3_length = group3_names.length;
```

```
// Populate Group4's Arrays

group4_names[0] = 'Group4_product one';
group4_locations[0] = 'group4/prod_1.html';

group4_names[1] = 'Group4_product two';
group4_locations[1] = 'group4/prod_2.html';

group4_names[2] = 'Group4_product three';
group4_locations[2] = 'group4/prod_3.html';

group4_names[3] = 'Group4_product four';
group4_locations[3] = 'group4/prod_4.html';

group4_names[4] = 'Group4_product five';
group4_locations[4] = 'group4/prod_5.html';

var group4_length = group4_names.length;
```

Now we have two arrays for each product group populated with the data for all of the products within those groups. We also have four variables that contain the lengths of each of the arrays. With this done, it's time to move on to the next step—creating the function that will populate our second pull-down menu.

Creating the Drill-Down Menu Function

Before we begin writing the function, we need to find a value inside the function. When the user selects a product group from the first menu, the script will have to clear out any values that are currently occupying the second menu before it inserts the new products. This is important because the new product group the user picks could have fewer products than the one that was previously chosen. If this were the case, the new group's products may not overwrite all of the products from the previous group. To make sure we clear all of the possible products from the menu, we will need the length of the largest set of arrays. We accomplish this with the following code:

```
// Find the length of the largest set of arrays

var maxLength = group1_length;

if (group2_length > maxLength)
{
    maxlength = group2_length;
}
```

```
if (group3_length > maxLength)
{
     maxlength = group3_length;
}
if (group4_length > maxLength)
{
     maxlength = group4_length;
}
```

This code first assigns the value of the length of the first set of arrays to the variable maxLength. It then uses if statements to check if the lengths of any of the other array groups are longer than maxLength, and then assigns that new value to the variable. In the end, maxLength is left holding the value of the longest array group.

Now we can move on to our function. The first thing we need to do is use our maxLength variable to clear the contents of the second menu.

```
// Creating the drill-down menu function

function MenuFiller(choice)
{

     // Clear out second menu
     var currentPosition = 0;
     while (currentPosition < maxLength)
     {
          . . .
          ++currentPosition;
     }
     . . .
}
```

The first line of the preceding code creates a variable currentPosition and assigns it a value of 0. Next, we have a structure called a while loop. We haven't used a while loop yet, so a quick look at its syntax is in order.

We have already used if statements in our scripts—they execute a chunk of code if a specific condition is true. While loops work in a similar fashion; however, they will continue to execute the code chunk they contain for as long as a specific condition evaluates true. The syntax for a while loop is as follows:

```
while (condition)
{
     statements
}
```

While loops are very useful when you want to access or change many properties in the same way. Loops can be tricky, though; if you create a loop where the condition will always be true, you will find yourself in something called an "infinite" loop. In other words, your script will be stuck running forever and will never be able to finish, which renders your script useless, and more often than not will crash the browser.

How do you change the condition you are testing to false if you can't leave the loop until it changes? We're glad you asked. The most common solution is to change the condition from within the loop.

The while loop in the preceding code will cycle through for as long as the variable currentPosition is less than the value of maxLength. Each time the loop cycles we will have it first clear out the menu option whose position corresponds to the value of currentPosition, and then at the end have it add 1 to the value of currentPosition. This way, currentPositionwill eventually equal maxLength and we will exit the loop. This is also the first time we have seen the ++ increment operator, which adds 1 to the value of its operand (in this case, currentPosition). Therefore, the line

```
++currentPosition;
```

is responsible for incrementing our variable.

The loop will cycle until the value of currentPosition is equal to the length of the longest array. This way, we will be sure to clear out all of the possible options from the menu. We accomplish the actual clearing of the menu by putting the following code into the while loop:

```
// Creating the drill-down menu function

function MenuFiller(choice)
{

    // Clear out second menu
    var currentPosition = 0;
    while (currentPosition < maxLength)
    {
        document.ProductPicker
        .Products.options[currentPosition].text = ' ' ;

        document.ProductPicker
        .Products.options[test].value = ' ' ;

        ++currentPosition;
    }
```

```
        . . .
    }
```

The first line of code we have inserted will set the text of the menu options, which correspond to the present value of the variable `currentPosition`, to be blank. The second line does the same with the value of that menu option. Once the loop has run through all of its cycles, we will be left with a blank pull-down menu ready to accept the values of the new product group.

Now that we have cleared out the Products menu, it's time to start populating it with the products of the new product group that was chosen. Before we can know what products to put there, we have to find out which product the user chose. As in our previous projects, we will have the event handler pass a value into the function that we can use to check which option has been chosen. For this function the value will be stored in the variable `choice`. The next chunk of code that we add will be a set of `if` statements to test which group was chosen:

```
// Creating the drill-down menu function

function MenuFiller(choice)
{

    // Clear out second menu
    var currentPosition = 0;
    while (currentPosition < maxLength)
    {
        document.ProductPicker
        .Products.options[currentPosition].text = ' ' ;

        document.ProductPicker
        .Products.options[test].value = ' ' ;

        ++currentPosition;
    }

    // Select which Product Group was chosen
    if (choice == 0)
    {
        . . .
    }
    else if (choice == 1)
    {
        . . .
    }
    else if (choice == 2)
    {
        . . .
```

```
    }
    else if (choice == 3)
    {
        . . .
    }
    else if (choice == 4)
    {
        . . .
    }
    . . .
}
```

If you look at the HTML code for our pull-down menus, you will see that the values we have given to the product groups are the numbers 1 through 4, with each number corresponding to the number of the group:

```
<SELECT NAME="ProductGroup">
    <OPTION VALUE="0">Choose a Group
    <OPTION VALUE="1">Group One
    <OPTION VALUE="2">Group Two
    <OPTION VALUE="3">Group Three
    <OPTION VALUE="4">Group Four
</SELECT>

<SELECT NAME="Products">
    <OPTION VALUE=" ">Choose a
    Group      
    <OPTION VALUE=" "> 
    <OPTION VALUE=" "> 
    <OPTION VALUE=" "> 
    <OPTION VALUE=" "> 
    <OPTION VALUE=" "> 
</SELECT>
```

Because it is possible that someone will choose the default menu entry Choose a Group, we have assigned a value of 0 to that choice. When the event handler is put into action, it passes the chosen value into the function, assigns it to the variable choice, and the if statements we just added will execute the commands that follow the test that proves true.

Let's put in the commands that we want executed after all of the if statements. These commands need to accomplish two things: They must assign the length of the chosen group's Products array to a variable, and then assign the name of the chosen group to a variable.

```
// Creating the drill-down menu function

function MenuFiller(choice)
```

```
{
        // Clear out second menu
        var currentPosition = 0;
        while (currentPosition < maxLength)
        {
                document.ProductPicker
                .Products.options[currentPosition].text = ' ' ;

                document.ProductPicker
                .Products.options[test].value = ' ' ;

                ++currentPosition;
        }


        // Select which Product Group was chosen
        if (choice == 0)
        {
                ...
        }
        else if (choice == 1)
        {
                OutputListSize = group1_length;
                arrayName = "group1";
        }
        else if (choice == 2)
        {
                OutputListSize = group2_length;
                arrayName = "group2";
        }
        else if (choice == 3)
        {
                OutputListSize = group3_length;
                arrayName = "group3";
        }
        else if (choice == 4)
        {
                OutputListSize = group4_length;
                arrayName = "group4";
        }
        ...
}
```

We have already determined the lengths of the individual arrays earlier in this script and assigned them to different variables, such as group1_length, group2_length, and so forth. Using these values later in our function will require having a single variable that will hold the array length of just the group that was chosen. Therefore, in the preceding lines of code, we are assigning the array length of the chosen group to the variable OutputListSize.

The second line that we have added to each if statement will assign the name of the group, if it was chosen, to the variable arrayName. This variable will be used later to help call information from the proper array.

So far, we have taken care of the code for all of the if statements except for the first one, which will be true if the user has chosen the default Choose a Group menu option. Because this option doesn't correspond to any product group, there are no Product arrays to refill the second menu and we don't need to worry about finding an array length or the name of the product group. There is something that we want to do if this option is chosen; because the second menu is automatically wiped clean when the function is run, we will need to repopulate the default option of the menu with the text of Choose a Group. Therefore, we will add the following command, which will explicitly assign the value to the text property of the first option of the second menu. A second command, which will select the first option of the menu, is also added to the script.

```
// Creating the drill-down menu function

function MenuFiller(choice)
{
    // Clear out second menu
    var currentPosition = 0;
    while (currentPosition < maxLength)
    {
        document.ProductPicker
        .Products.options[currentPosition].text = ' ';

        document.ProductPicker
        .Products.options[currentPosition].value = ' ';

        ++currentPosition;
    }

    // Choose which Product Group was chosen
    if (choice == 0)
    {
        document.ProductPicker
        .Products.options[0].text = 'Choose a Group  ';

        document.ProductPicker
        .Products.options[0].selected=true;
    }
    else if (choice == 1)
```

```
{
     OutputListSize = group1_length;
     arrayName = "group1";
}
else if (choice == 2)
{
     OutputListSize = group2_length;
     arrayName = "group2";
}
else if (choice == 3)
{
     OutputListSize = group3_length;
     arrayName = "group3";
}
else if (choice == 4)
{
     OutputListSize = group4_length;
     arrayName = "group4";
}
```

We now have all of the information we will need to repopulate the second menu with the products from the chosen group. Let's move on to the final section of our function, which will actually do the repopulating. The first thing we need to do is reset the value of the variable `currentPosition` to 0 and make sure that the default `Choose a Group` option wasn't selected. If it was, we won't want to repopulate the menu, so we will use an `if` statement to make sure that `choice` is greater than 0.

```
// Creating the drill-down menu function

function MenuFiller(choice)
{
     // Clear out second menu
     var currentPosition = 0;
     while (currentPosition < maxLength)
     {
          document.ProductPicker.Products
          .options[currentPosition].text = ' ';

          document.ProductPicker.Products
          .options[currentPosition].value = ' ';

          ++currentPosition;
     }

     // Choose which Product Group was chosen
     if (choice == 0)
```

```
        {
                document.ProductPicker
                .Products.options[0].text = 'Choose a Group    ';

                document.ProductPicker.Products
                .options[0].selected=true;
        }
        else if (choice == 1)
        {
                OutputListSize = group1_length;
                arrayName = "group1";
        }
        else if (choice == 2)
        {
                OutputListSize = group2_length;
                arrayName = "group2";
        }
        else if (choice == 3)
        {
                OutputListSize = group3_length;
                arrayName = "group3";
        }
        else if (choice == 4)
        {
                OutputListSize = group4_length;
                arrayName = "group4";
        }

        var currentPosition = 0;

        if (choice > 0)
        {
                . . .
        }
}
```

Now that we know that a new product group has actually been chosen, we can start repopulating the second menu. We will use a `while` loop similar to the one that clears the menu at the beginning of the function. It will test the value of `currentPosition` against the variable `OutputListSize`, which contains the length of the chosen `Product` arrays.

```
var currentPosition = 0;
        if (choice > 0)
        {
                while (currentPosition < OutputListSize)
                {
                        . . .
```

```
                    ++currentPosition;
            }
    ...
        }
    }
```

Of course, the statements inside the loop will be different. To repopulate both the text and value properties of each menu option we will need to put in two lines of code for the `while` loop to execute.

```
var currentPosition = 0;
    if (choice > 0)
    {
        while (currentPosition < OutputListSize)
        {
            document.ProductPicker
            .Products.options[currentPosition]
            .text = eval(arrayName +
            '_names[currentPosition]');

            document.ProductPicker
            .Products.options[currentPosition]
            .value = eval(arrayName +
            '_locations[currentPosition]');

            ++currentPosition;
        }
        ...
    }
}
```

There is a lot going on in the preceding lines, so let's take a closer look at them. In the first half of the first line, we are calling the text property of the menu option that currently matches the value of the variable `currentPosition`.

```
document.ProductPicker.Products.options[currentPosition]
.text
```

Each time the `while` loop cycles through, this property will be assigned the value of what it finds in the second half of the line.

```
= eval(arrayName + '_names[currentPosition]');
```

This part of the line is similar to one that we used in Chapter 2, when we dealt with image rollovers. Here we are using the `eval()` method to combine the value of the variable `arrayName`, which holds the name of the group that was chosen and a string, which, when combined, will call on the proper Product array and retrieve the entry at the position that corresponds to the current value of currentPosition.

While the first line takes care of repopulating the text property of the option in the pull-down menu, the second line repopulates the value property of each menu option.

The last command that we need to add to our function will make sure that the first position on the repopulated second menu is the one that is selected by default.

```
var currentPosition = 0;
    if (choice > 0)
    {
        while (currentPosition < OutputListSize)
        {
            document.ProductPicker
            .Products.options[currentPosition].text =
            eval(arrayName +
            '_names[currentPosition]');

            document.ProductPicker
            .Products.options[currentPosition]
            .value = eval(arrayName +
            '_locations[currentPosition]');

            ++currentPosition;
        }
        document.ProductPicker
        .Products.options[0].selected=true;
    }
}
```

Congratulations, we have finished our function. This is definitely an advanced piece of code, so be proud of yourself. Only two more steps to go and we will have completed the project. Next, we must add the navigation function that will take the user to the page of the product that he or she chooses, and then insert the event handlers that will call our function.

Creating the Navigation Function

Now we need a function that will send the user to a different page depending on which item he or she chooses from the Products pull-down menu. Wait, does this sound familiar to anyone else? Well, it should—we created just such a function at the beginning of this chapter. With a little modification we can use that existing function for both the quick-link navigation and for our Products pull-down menu.

When the page is first loaded and the user has not yet chosen a product group, the Products pull-down menu is empty and will stay that way until a group is chosen. The addition we need to make to the function is a test that will make sure that any option chosen from the Products pull-down menu will be populated with data. If it's not, we don't want the Navigation Function to send the person to some nonexistent page.

Here is a look at the existing function just to refresh your memory:

```
// Pull-Down Menu Navigation Function

function PageChanger(page)
{
    document.location= page;
    document.NavForm.PullDown.options[0].selected=true;
}
```

We can use the value of the menu option, which is being passed into the function, to make our test. We will insert an if statement that tells the JavaScript runtime engine to execute the rest of the function if the value of variable page is not equal to (!=) a blank entry.

```
// Pull-Down Menu Navigation Function

function PageChanger(page)
{
    if (page != ' ')
    {
        document.location= page;
        document.NavForm.PullDown
        .options[0].selected=true;
    }
}
```

With the addition of one simple if statement, we're able to repurpose an existing function. Keep this trick in mind when you are coding—there is no reason to always reinvent the wheel.

Now that we have a function sending the user where he or she wants to go, all that is left for us to do is put in the event handlers.

Inserting the Event Handlers

There are two event handlers that we need to insert—one for each of our pull-down menus. The Product Group pull-down menu will call our MenuFiller() function, while the Products pull-down menu will call the PageChanger() function. Let's look at the Product Group pull-down menu first:

```
<SELECT NAME="ProductGroup"
onChange="MenuFiller(this.options[this.selectedIndex]
.value)">
     <OPTION value="0">Choose a Group
     <OPTION VALUE="1">Group One
     <OPTION VALUE="2">Group Two
     <OPTION VALUE="3">Group Three
     <OPTION VALUE="4">Group Four
</SELECT>
```

The event handler should look familiar. For the most part, it's the
same as the handler that we used for our navigation pull-down menu
at the beginning of the chapter. The only difference is that we are calling a different function. Therefore, we will use the same event handler:

```
<SELECT NAME="Products"
onChange="PageChanger(this.options[this.selectedIndex]
.value)">
     <OPTION VALUE=" ">Choose a
     Group      
     <OPTION VALUE=" "> 
     <OPTION VALUE=" "> 
     <OPTION VALUE=" "> 
     <OPTION VALUE=" "> 
     <OPTION VALUE=" "> 
</SELECT>
```

Believe it or not, that's it; we are now finished. This is definitely
the longest script we have worked on so far, so let's review it one last
time as a whole and see exactly what we have accomplished.

REVIEWING THE SCRIPT

The first thing we did in this script was to define the arrays that would
hold all of the information for the products of each product group:

```
// Arrays for Products

    //Define the arrays

group1_names = new Array(5);
group1_locations = new Array(5);

group2_names = new Array(5);
group2_locations = new Array(5);
```

```
group3_names = new Array(5);
group3_locations = new Array(5);

group4_names = new Array(5);
group4_locations = new Array(5);
```

1. We created two arrays for each product group: One set of arrays will hold the product names for each group, and the other will hold the URLs that correspond to each product.

Once we created the arrays, our next step was to populate them with the product information.

```
// Populate Group1's Arrays

group1_names[0] = 'Group1_product one';
group1_locations[0] = 'group1/prod_1.html';

group1_names[1] = 'Group1_product two';
group1_locations[1] = 'group1/prod_2.html';

group1_names[2] = 'Group1_product three';
group1_locations[2] = 'group1/prod_3.html';

group1_names[3] = 'Group1_product four';
group1_locations[3] = 'group1/prod_4.html';

group1_names[4] = 'Group1_product five';
group1_locations[4] = 'group1/prod_5.html';

var group1_length = group1_names.length;


// Populate Group2's Arrays

group2_names[0] = 'Group2_product one';
group2_locations[0] = 'group2/prod_1.html';

group2_names[1] = 'Group2_product two';
group2_locations[1] = 'group2/prod_2.html';

group2_names[2] = 'Group2_product three';
group2_locations[2] = 'group2/prod_3.html';

group2_names[3] = 'Group2_product four';
group2_locations[3] = 'group2/prod_4.html';

group2_names[4] = 'Group2_product five';
group2_locations[4] = 'group2/prod_5.html';
```

```
var group2_length = group2_names.length;


// Populate Group3's Arrays

group3_names[0] = 'Group3_product one';
group3_locations[0] = 'group3/prod_1.html';

group3_names[1] = 'Group3_product two';
group3_locations[1] = 'group3/prod_2.html';

group3_names[2] = 'Group3_product three';
group3_locations[2] = 'group3/prod_3.html';

group3_names[3] = 'Group3_product four';
group3_locations[3] = 'group3/prod_4.html';

group3_names[4] = 'Group3_product five';
group3_locations[4] = 'group3/prod_5.html';

var group3_length = group3_names.length;


// Populate Group4's Arrays

group4_names[0] = 'Group4_product one';
group4_locations[0] = 'group4/prod_1.html';

group4_names[1] = 'Group4_product two';
group4_locations[1] = 'group4/prod_2.html';

group4_names[2] = 'Group4_product three';
group4_locations[2] = 'group4/prod_3.html';

group4_names[3] = 'Group4_product four';
group4_locations[3] = 'group4/prod_4.html';

group4_names[4] = 'Group4_product five';
group4_locations[4] = 'group4/prod_5.html';

var group4_length = group4_names.length;
```

2. With all of the arrays populated, we created a variable for each group that would hold the length of each group's arrays.

```
// Find the length of the largest set of arrays

var maxLength = group1_length;
```

```
if (group2_length > maxLength)
{
     maxlength = group2_length;
}
if (group3_length > maxLength)
{
     maxlength = group3_length;
}
if (group4_length > maxLength)
{
     maxlength = group4_length;
}
```

3. Once we had the lengths of all of the arrays stored in the variables, we set up a series of `if` statements to find the longest of the groups and assigned that length to the variable `maxLength`.

Next, we created the function `MenuFiller()` that will populate the pull-down menus.

```
// Creating the drill-down menu function

function MenuFiller(choice)
{
     // Clear out second menu
     var currentPosition = 0;
     while (currentPosition < maxLength)
     {
          document.ProductPicker
          .Products.options[currentPosition].text = ' ' ;

          document.ProductPicker
          .Products.options[currentPosition].value = ' ' ;

          ++currentPosition;
     }

     // Choose which Product Group was chosen
     if (choice == 0)
     {
          document.ProductPicker
          .Products.options[0].text = 'Choose a Group  ';

          document.ProductPicker
          .Products.options[0].value = ' ';

          document.ProductPicker
          .Products.options[0].selected=true;
     }
```

```
else if (choice == 1)
{
    OutputListSize = group1_length;
    arrayName = "group1";
}
else if (choice == 2)
{
    OutputListSize = group2_length;
    arrayName = "group2";
}
else if (choice == 3)
{
    OutputListSize = group3_length;
    arrayName = "group3";
}
else if (choice == 4)
{
    OutputListSize = group4_length;
    arrayName = "group4";
}

var currentPosition = 0;
if (choice > 0)
{
    while (currentPosition < OutputListSize)
    {
        document.ProductPicker
        .Products.options[currentPosition]
        .text = eval(arrayName +
        '_names[currentPosition]');

        document.ProductPicker
        .Products.options[currentPosition]
        .value = eval(arrayName +
        '_locations[currentPosition]');

        ++currentPosition;
    }
    document.ProductPicker
    .Products.options[0].selected=true;
}
}
```

1. First, we had our function clear out any data from the Products pull-down menu.

2. Then, the function took the variable passed into it from the event handler and decided which Product group the user chose.

3. Finally, our function repopulated the Products pull-down menu with the information from the proper array.

With that function complete, we made a quick adjustment to the existing Navigation Function.

```
// Pull-Down Menu Navigation Function

function PageChanger(page)
{
    if (page != ' ')
    {
        document.location= page;
        document.NavForm
        .PullDown.options[0].selected=true;
    }
}
```

1. Here we have added an if statement to our PageChanger() function to make sure that the option chosen from the pull-down menu is valid.

Finally, we added event handlers to our two Product pull-downs.

```
<SELECT NAME="ProductGroup"
onChange="MenuFiller(this.options[this.selectedIndex]
.value)">
    <OPTION value="0">Choose a Group
    <OPTION VALUE="1">Group One
    <OPTION VALUE="2">Group Two
    <OPTION VALUE="3">Group Three
    <OPTION VALUE="4">Group Four
</SELECT>

<SELECT NAME="Products"
onChange="PageChanger(this.options[this.selectedIndex]
.value)">
    <OPTION VALUE=" ">Choose a
    Group      
    <OPTION VALUE=" "> 
    <OPTION VALUE=" "> 
    <OPTION VALUE=" "> 
    <OPTION VALUE=" "> 
    <OPTION VALUE=" "> 
</SELECT>
```

2. We inserted an onChange event handler into our two pull-down menus.

The event handler in the Product Group pull-down menu will call our MenuFiller() function.

The event handler in the Products pull-down menu will call the PageChanger() function.

Let's look at the new concepts we have covered in this project:

- Creating and populating user-defined arrays.
- The `while` loop.
- The `!=` logical operator.
- Accessing the information and properties contained in arrays.
- Accessing and changing the values and properties of form elements.

Now that we are finished, it's time to hand the work over to the boss so he can lavish you with much deserved praise. You're becoming a downright JavaScript guru. Of course, now that you have finished this project, the boss has found another one for you to work on. Geez, our work is never done.

◆ Project III: Using JavaScript on a Log-in Page

Shelley Biotech is about to add a new Partners section to the site. Part of this new section will not be accessible to the general public; only existing partners will be allowed entry. Some of the Perl programmers have created a log-in page (see Figure 3–4), written the script, and are going to maintain the database with usernames and passwords. So, what is there for you to do, you ask?

Well, the powers that be want a log-in page that allows the user to enter a password, and then press Enter to call the log-in script. The log-in page that the Perl guys came up with requires the user to manually press a log-in button to call the script. Our job is to take the page they created and modify it with JavaScript so that it will work when the Enter key is pressed.

After our last script, this is going to seem like a walk in the park. We won't even need to write a function; all we need to do is insert the proper event handler in the HTML and we will be off and running.

Inserting the Event Handler

In our last two scripts in this chapter we used the `onChange()` event handler on form pull-down menus to call the functions needed to run the scripts. For this script, we will be using `onChange()` again; however, this time we will see how it works on a form text field.

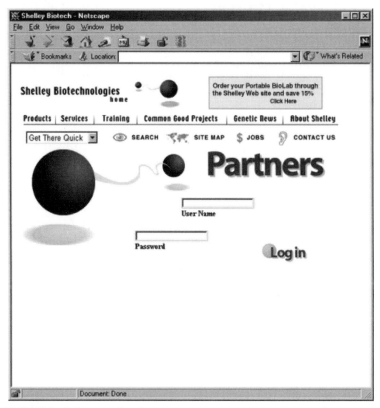

FIGURE 3–4 Partners log-in page

When the onChange() handler is placed within a text field of a form, it is activated when the user changes the value held within the field and then either presses the Tab or Enter key or clicks the cursor outside the field. This causes the text field to lose focus, which then triggers the event handler. In this script we will be putting the onChange() handler in the password field. When a user visits the page, he or she will first enter a username and then move to the Password field. The user will enter a password, thereby changing the value of the field and then either press Enter or click the Log-in button, which will cause the Password field to lose focus and trigger the event. The event we are going to have triggered is the calling of the SUBMIT property of the form that holds our log-in text fields.

Let's look at the code after we have inserted the event handler:

```
<INPUT TYPE="password" NAME="_User_Pass"
onChange="document.login.submit();">
```

REVIEWING THE SCRIPT

1. We inserted the `onChange()` event handler into the `password` form element.

That's all there is to it. This is a great example of a very short script that can be really useful. Not all scripts have to be as long or as complex as the second one in this chapter. In fact, it is best to always look for the most efficient way to create a script.

RECAP

You should now have a good understanding of how to use JavaScript for navigation, as well as in forms for enhanced interactivity and efficiency. We have also broadened our knowledge of arrays, learning how to create them and access information that we have stored in them. In the next chapter, we will leave the Shelley Biotech site and start working on *Stitch Magazine*'s site. We will be building on what we have learned about JavaScript and forms, and learn how to handle error checking with JavaScript.

ADVANCED PROJECTS

1. Create a system of three pull-down menus, where the second menu populates based on the choice made from the first menu, and the third menu then populates based on the choice made from the second menu.

2. Create a system of three pull-down menus, where the choice made from the first menu then dynamically populates the other two menus.

4 Error Handling in Forms

IN THIS CHAPTER

- Project I: Checking for Empty Form Fields
- Project II: Checking for Erroneous Data in Form Fields
- Project III: Letting the User Know What's Wrong
- Recap
- Advanced Projects

In the second half of the book, we will be working on the Web site of Stitch Magazine—a fictional online fashion magazine. It's racy, visually interesting, and its reporters are remarkably good at spotting trends, tracking down reclusive designers, and unearthing embarrassing gossip. However, the magazine is beginning to grow up and needs more interactivity to enhance its Web site content. In the next two chapters, we'll use JavaScript to affect changes in other frames and implement some truly advanced JavaScript for a rare user experience. In this chapter, we'll learn how to check forms for user-entered errors.

The marketing folks at Stitch are running a promotion to generate some leads. To enter the contest, Web surfers must visit the Stitch Web site and enter some information about themselves in a form (for example, their name, e-mail address, and what they want to know about fashion).

Chances are that most people will enter the information correctly. However, some will mistype their responses, some will skip information the marketing folks desperately need, and some will fill in the form with garbage.

If you include some JavaScript to error-check the form before it's submitted to a CGI script, the marketing people will have less incomplete or nonsensical data to sort through. Error checking will also make the CGI programmer's life easier because you can guarantee that the data will arrive in certain forms. This is a pretty lengthy script, so we will break it up into three projects: First, we will check for empty form fields. Then, we will check for erroneous data entered by the user, and, finally, we will discuss how to let the user know what is wrong. Because all of these projects are really part of the same script, we will review each part at the end of the chapter when we have the completed script.

◆ Project I: Checking for Empty Form Fields

The marketing folks want users to fill in all of the boxes on the form, but only a few pieces of data are truly necessary to generate a lead (see Figure 4–1). Generally, you should stick with the name and e-mail address as required entries. Avoid requiring a phone number unless it's absolutely necessary—people will assume you're going to sic a telemarketer on them and they may enter in the phone number of their ex-significant other instead.

Here is the form that *Stitch's* HTML programmers put together:

```
<FORM ACTION="/scripts/promotion.cgi" NAME="promotion"
METHOD="post">
Fields with a <B><FONT COLOR="#FF0000">*</FONT></B> are
required fields.
<P>
<TABLE BORDER="0">
<TR>
    <TD><B><FONT COLOR="#FF0000">*</FONT></B></TD>
    <TD><B>First Name</B></TD>
    <TD><INPUT TYPE="text" NAME="firstName"></TD>
</TR>
<TR>
    <TD><B><FONT COLOR="#FF0000">*</FONT></B></TD>
    <TD><B>Last Name</B></TD>
    <TD><INPUT TYPE="text" NAME="lastName"></TD>
</TR>
```

```
</TABLE>
<TABLE BORDER="0">
<TR>
    <TD COLSPAN="3">
        <B>Mailing Address</B>
    </TD>
</TR>
<TR>
    <TD> </TD>
    <TD><B>Street</B></TD>
    <TD><INPUT TYPE="text" SIZE="40" NAME="address"></TD>
</TR>
<TR>
    <TD> </TD>
    <TD><B>City</TD>
    <TD><INPUT TYPE="text" NAME="address">  
        <B>State</B><INPUT TYPE="text" NAME="address"
        MAXLENGTH="2" SIZE="2">  <B>Zip
        Code</B><INPUT TYPE="text" NAME="zipCode"
        MAXLENGTH="5" SIZE="5">
    </TD>
</TR>
</TABLE>
<TABLE>
<TR>
    <TD><B><FONT COLOR="#FF0000">*</FONT></B></TD>
    <TD><B>Email Address</B></TD>
    <TD><INPUT TYPE="text" NAME="email"></TD>
</TR>
<TR>
    <TD> </TD>
    <TD><B>Phone Number</B></TD>
    <TD>
        <INPUT TYPE="text" NAME="phonenumber" SIZE="12"
        MAXLENGTH="12">
    </TD>
</TR>
<TR>
    <TD> </TD>
    <TD><B>Fax Number</B></TD>
    <TD>
        <INPUT TYPE="text" NAME="faxnumber" SIZE="123"
        MAXLENGTH="12">
    </TD>
</TR>
<TR>
    <TD> </TD>
    <TD><B>What interests you most<BR>
        about clothes and fashion?</B>
```

```
        </TD>
        <TD>
            <TEXTAREA ROWS="6" COLS="40">Be honest</TEXTAREA>
        </TD>
    </TR>
    <TR>
        <TD><B><FONT COLOR="#FF0000">*</FONT></B></TD>
        <TD>
            <B>What do you want to see in an<BR>
               online fashion magazine like Stitch?</B>
        </TD>
        <TD>
            <SELECT NAME="whatTheyWant">
            <OPTION VALUE="">Please choose a category
            <OPTION VALUE="trends">Upcoming trends
            <OPTION VALUE="models">Information about
             models
            <OPTION VALUE="designers">Information about
             designers
            <OPTION VALUE="rage">What the current rage is
            <OPTION VALUE="gossip">Gossip!
            </SELECT>
        </TD>
    </TR>
    <TR>
        <TD COLSPAN="2">Want to join?</TD>
        <TD><INPUT TYPE="checkbox" NAME="join" SELECTED></TD>
    </TR>
    <TR>
        <TD COLSPAN="2">
            <INPUT TYPE="button" VALUE="Click to Submit"
            onClick="errorCheck()">
        </TD>
    </TR>
    </TABLE>
    </FORM>
```

You will notice that at the end of the form the programmers have already inserted an `onClick` event handler into the Submit button, within which they are calling the `errorCheck()` function. Since they went to the trouble of putting in the handler, we will use it for the name of the function that we will be creating.

Checking Forms for Empty Text Box Fields

Following is the first bit of JavaScript we'll be using to check the visitor's information:

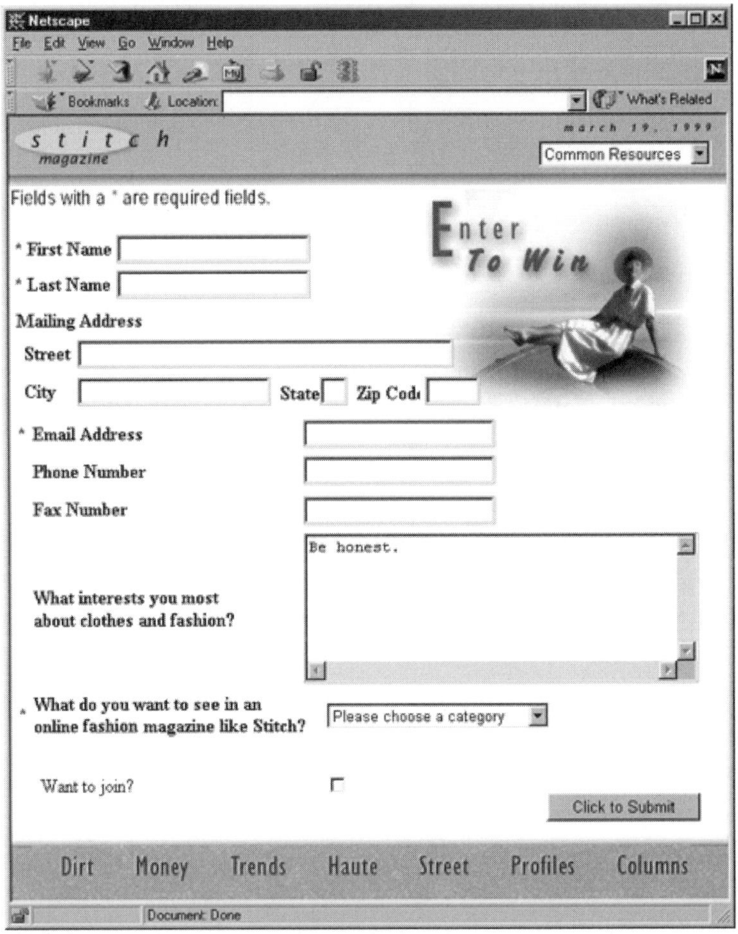

FIGURE 4-1 *Stitch* promotion form page

```
<SCRIPT LANGUAGE = "JavaScript">
<!-- Code after this will be ignored by older browsers


//Create the errorCheck Function
function errorCheck()
{
    // Create some variables for our script
    var requiredFieldsErrorMessage = "";
    var firstNameEntered = "";
    var lastNameEntered = "";
    var emailEntered = "";
```

```
    var areaCodeEntered = "";
    var zipCodeEntered = "";
    var pullDownErrorMessage = "";
    var emailErrorMessage = "";
    var areaCodeErrorMessage = "";
    var zipCodeErrorMessage = "";
    ...
}


// Stop hiding the code here -->
</SCRIPT>
```

In the preceding code, we set some variables. We will use the first four in this project and the others will be used in subsequent projects. These variables will keep track of any specific error messages the user generates. At the end of the script, all the error messages will be patched together and one comprehensive error message will greet the site's visitor.

Next, we will begin to add the part of the function that will check the information.

```
<SCRIPT LANGUAGE = "JavaScript">
<!-- Code after this will be ignored by older browsers

//Create the errorCheck Function
function errorCheck()
{
    // Create some variables for our script
    var requiredFieldsErrorMessage = "";
    var firstNameEntered = "";
    var lastNameEntered = "";
    var emailEntered = "";
    var areaCodeEntered = "";
    var zipCodeEntered = "";
    var pullDownErrorMessage = "";
    var emailErrorMessage = "";;
    var areaCodeErrorMessage = "";
    var zipCodeErrorMessage = "";

    // Required fields error checking
    firstNameEntered = document.forms['promotion']
    .elements['firstName'].value

    lastNameEntered = document.forms['promotion']
    .elements['lastName'].value

    emailEntered = document.forms['promotion']
    .elements['email'].value
```

```
      . . .
}
// Stop hiding the code here -->
</SCRIPT>
```

We're requiring the visitor to enter information in three fields: first name, last name, and e-mail address. In previous chapters, we learned how to access values from FORM elements on an HTML page. Here we're going to use similar methods to get the values for the three fields we need to check. Thus, the line

```
firstNameEntered =
document.forms['promotion'].elements['firstName'].value
```

looks at what the visitor entered into the text field for first name and puts that value into the variable firstNameEntered. This line is followed by similar statements for the other two fields. If the user didn't input any information for these three questions, the variables would be empty. Next, we'll set up an if statement to test these values.

```
<SCRIPT LANGUAGE = "JavaScript">
<!-- Code after this will be ignored by older browsers

//Create the errorCheck Function
function errorCheck()
{
      // Create some variables for our script
      var requiredFieldsErrorMessage = "";
      var firstNameEntered = "";
      var lastNameEntered = "";
      var emailEntered = "";
      var areaCodeEntered = "";
      var zipCodeEntered = "";
      var pullDownErrorMessage = "";
      var emailErrorMessage = "";
      var areaCodeErrorMessage = "";
      var zipCodeErrorMessage = "";

      // Required fields error checking
      firstNameEntered = document.forms['promotion']
      .elements['firstName'].value

      lastNameEntered = document.forms['promotion']
      .elements['lastName'].value

      emailEntered = document.forms['promotion']
      .elements['email'].value
```

```
if ((!firstNameEntered) || (!lastNameEntered) ||
(!emailEntered))
{
      if (!firstNameEntered)
      {
            requiredFieldsErrorMessage = "- your
            first name\r"
      }
      if (!lastNameEntered)
      {
            requiredFieldsErrorMessage =
            requiredFieldsErrorMessage + "- your
            last name\r"
      }
      if (!emailEntered)
      {
            requiredFieldsErrorMessage =
            requiredFieldsErrorMessage + "- your
            email address\r"
      }
}
    . . .
}
// Stop hiding the code here -->
</SCRIPT>
```

The first line of the `if` statement is

```
if ((!firstNameEntered) || (!lastNameEntered) ||
(!emailEntered))
```

which tells the JavaScript runtime engine: If a visitor doesn't enter in a first name, last name, or e-mail address, then the `if` statement is `false`.

The double bar (`||`) is the symbol used for "or" in conditional statements. When using an "or" operator in a conditional statement such as an `if` statement, if any of the conditions are met then the `if` is seen as `true` and the statements that follow are executed. We have also used the `!` operator in the preceding `if` statement. In JavaScript (and most other programming languages) this is the "not" symbol. Therefore, the preceding line of code tells the engine to return a value of `true` if a variable does not have a value. The engine will then go on to execute the next statements. If all three fields were filled out correctly, our script will just skip ahead to the code following our `if` statement.

Chances are good that all three fields will not be filled out correctly, so we put in some code that will be executed if there are any errors. We added three more `if` statements that will test the three fields individually and, if necessary, store a short message in the `requiredFieldsErrorMessage` variable that we will use later to tell the user that a field has been missed.

```
if (!firstNameEntered)
```

The preceding `if` statement means that if the visitor didn't enter a first name, the next line is executed:

```
requiredFieldsErrorMessage = "- your first name\r";
```

This line assigns the string `"- your first name"` to the variable `requiredFieldsErrorMessage`. You will notice the `\r` at the end of the string—as stated in previous chapters the backward slash escapes the character that follows it and tells the JavaScript engine to execute it. The `r` value tells the engine to insert a line break, similar to pressing the Enter key.

There are two more `if` statements that check for the presence of a value in the two other fields we are concerned with, and that will add information to the `requiredFieldsErrorMessage` variable if they are empty.

```
requiredFieldsErrorMessage = requiredFieldsErrorMessage
+ "- your last name\r";
```

The preceding statement is executed if the last name test comes back empty. We want to add to the visitor's existing error message because he or she may make more than one error. Therefore, on the right-hand side of the expression, the script is telling the engine to add `your last name\r` to the existing value for `requiredFields-ErrorMessage` and then put them both back into the `required-FieldsErrorMessage` variable. If more than one mistake is made, we want to list both of them, not just replace the first mistake with the next one. The third `while` loop follows the same syntax, and checks for the presence of a value in the e-mail address field.

Making Sure a Pull-Down Menu Option Was Chosen

Next, we have to make sure that an option was chosen from the pull-down menu that asks what the user wants to see in an online version of the magazine. Fortunately, the code that we will use to do this is very similar to the code that we have already used to check the values of text fields that hold the user's name. We will insert the JavaScript code to check the pull-down menu following the code we created to test the text boxes.

```
//Checking for pull-down errors

if (document.forms['promotion'].elements['whatTheyWant']
.value == 'default')
{
    pullDownErrorMessage = "- you didn't tell us what
    you want to see in Stitch";
}
// Stop hiding the code here -->
</SCRIPT>
```

Because we are only checking for one form field, we can use just one `if` statement. In the preceding `if` statement, we are testing the value of the `whatTheyWant` field against the value `default`. If you look at the HTML code for the pull-down menu, you will see that `default` is the value assigned to the first option in the menu. Therefore, if the user doesn't change it from its initial position and pick another option, the value will remain `default`, and the script will then assign a short message to the variable `pullDownErrorMessage`.

So far, we have written a script that will test for empty fields in the form; however, there are cases where that is not enough information. In certain instances it would be useful to check for a bogus or erroneous response from the user. The next project will cover several examples of just such cases.

◆ Project II: Checking for Erroneous Data in Form Fields

Checking E-mail Addresses for Valid Characters

You can never be 100% sure that someone is giving you a working e-mail address. There's no formula or central database that keeps track of all the valid e-mail addresses in the world. However, you can be sure that a person is giving you something that at least *looks* like an e-mail address by checking for an @ symbol and a period. Even though we are treating this section as a new project, the code in this chapter is really all part of one script. We will add this new code after our existing code, which is still within the `errorCheck()` function.

```
// email error checking

if (emailEntered)
{
    emailEntered = document.forms['promotion']
    .elements['email'].value;

    emailValue = new String (emailEntered);
    emailHasAt = emailValue.indexOf("@");
    emailHasPeriod = emailValue.indexOf(".");

    if ((emailHasAt == -1) || (emailHasPeriod == -1))
    {
        emailErrorMessage = "-your email address\r";
    }
}
// Stop hiding the code here -->
</SCRIPT>
```

The first thing we've done here is to again harvest the value of the field in question and assign it to a variable. We then create a new object called emailValue—we do this the same way that we created the IMAGE objects we used in Chapter 2 for our image rollovers. Instead of creating an IMAGE object, however, we are creating a STRING object that will hold the value that is now in our emailEntered variable:

```
emailValue = new String (emailEntered);
```

The reason we are putting the field value into an object instead of simply keeping it in a regular variable as before is because objects are more versatile and allow us access to methods that we can't use on variables. We will be using the indexOf() method in this script. This lets us look for specific characters that appear in the string; in this case, we will be looking for the @ symbol and a period.

```
emailHasAt = emailValue.indexOf("@");
emailHasPeriod = emailValue.indexOf(".");
```

This first line looks for the character @ in the object emailValue and remembers where in the object that character occurred. For example, if emailValue was "dan@wire-man.com," the @ is in position 3 (remember, JavaScript starts counting with 0), then emailHasAt would hold the value 3. If that character isn't found, you get a value of –1.

The second line is basically the same but it is checking for the existence of a period and is storing its findings in the variable emailHasPeriod. Thus, the next lines

```
if ((emailHasAt == -1) || (emailHasPeriod == -1))
{
    emailErrorMessage = "-your email address\r";
}
```

tell the engine to create a new error message called email-ErrorMessage if the e-mail address didn't have an @ symbol or a period. Next, we'll check the phone number fields for an area code.

Checking for Area Codes in Phone Numbers

We're going to cheat a little bit here—we're going to reformat the HTML of the form so you only get the information you want from the phone field (see Figure 4–2). Keep this trick in mind when you are creating scripts later on—there are often ways in which you can manipulate the HTML to make your scripts more efficient. Here is the new HTML code for the phone number fields:

```
(<INPUT TYPE="text" NAME="areaCode" SIZE="3"
MAXLENGTH="3">)
<INPUT TYPE="text" NAME="phoneNumber1" SIZE="3"
MAXLENGTH="3">-
<INPUT TYPE="text" NAME="phoneNumber2" SIZE="4"
MAXLENGTH="4">
```

By separating the phone number into three different fields we can isolate the area code more easily. This way, you don't have to look at the entire phone number and try to figure out which part is the area code.

This can be a problem because people write area codes differently; for example, (925)555-1212, or 925-555-1212, or 925/555.1212, and so forth. Keep this in mind when writing scripts—there are often ways other than JavaScript solutions that are much easier to implement. Don't be afraid to explore these other avenues.

The phone number isn't a required field; however, if a visitor does volunteer a phone number, you want to make sure that he or she gives the area code; after all, this is the Web and you have no idea where people are calling from. (We're ignoring international phone numbers on purpose for now. If the Web site ends up getting a lot of hits from locations outside the U.S., we can change the phone number fields later.)

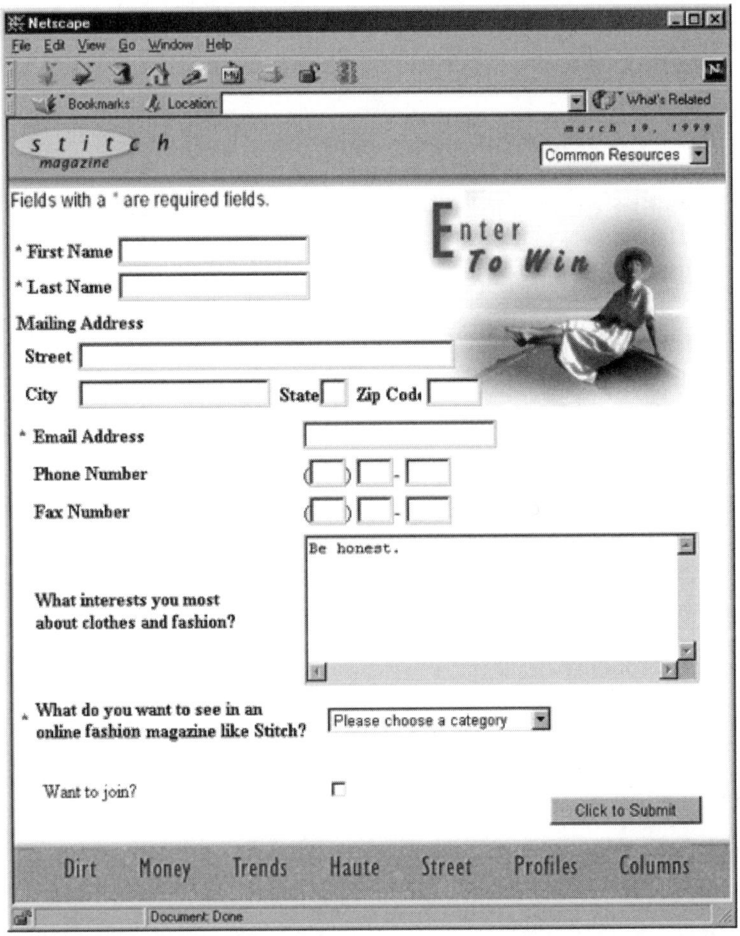

FIGURE 4–2 *Stitch* promotion form page with new phone number fields

Because we have decided to use three different fields for the phone number, we can check the values in much the same way as we checked for the first name, last name, and e-mail address fields.

```
// Area Code Check

areaCodeEntered =
document.forms['promotion'].elements['areaCode'].value

phoneNumber1Entered =
document.forms['promotion'].elements['phoneNumber1'].value
```

```
...
}
// Stop hiding the code here -->
</SCRIPT>
```

In the first two lines of the preceding code, we assigned the values of both the area code field and the first phone number field to variables. In the following lines, we will use an `if` statement to tell us if what we need is there.

```
// Area Code Check

areaCodeEntered =
document.forms['promotion'].elements['areaCode'].value

phoneNumber1Entered =
document.forms['promotion'].elements['phoneNumber1'].value

if ((!areaCodeEntered) && (phoneNumber1Entered))
{
    areaCodeErrorMessage = "-please enter your area
    code\r"
}
}
// Stop hiding the code here -->
</SCRIPT>
```

You haven't seen `&&` before, but it is another logical operator like the `||` operator that we used previously in the script. The `&&` operator means that both conditions need to be met to return a `true` value in the statement. Therefore,

```
if ((!areaCodeEntered) && (phoneNumberEntered))
```

tells the JavaScript runtime engine that if the variable `areaCode-Entered` has no value, but `phoneNumberEntered`does, then it should execute the next lines. This way, an error message is generated only if the visitor entered in a phone number without an area code. Now, let's move on to the final field that we have to test.

Making Sure Zip Codes Have Only Numbers

The JavaScript to make sure the visitor's zip code is just numbers is more complicated than what we've already seen, and introduces a number of new features and functions. The overall plan is to look at the five-character string contained in the variable `zipCodeEntered` one character at a time and see if each character is actually a number. If it is, then we set a variable to yes and move on to the next character. If, however, it finds a character that is not a number, then it will create an error message. This portion of the script begins like most of the others, by gathering the value of the field we need to check and assigning it to a variable.

```
// Zip Code Check

zipCodeEntered =
document.forms['promotion'].elements['zipCode'].value;
 . . .
}
// Stop hiding the code here -->
</SCRIPT>
```

Next, because it is not required for the user to put in an address, we will use an if statement to see if there is anything at all in the zip code field.

```
// Zip Code Check

zipCodeEntered =
document.forms['promotion'].elements['zipCode'].value;

if (zipCodeEntered)
{
 . . .
}
}
// Stop hiding the code here -->
</SCRIPT>
```

If there is no value in the zip code field, the script will ignore the rest of our zip code check and go on to the next part. However, if there is a value in the field, we will need to create some variables and assign some of them a base value, so that we can check for a proper zip code entry.

```
// Zip Code Check

zipCodeEntered =
document.forms['promotion'].elements['zipCode'].value;

if (zipCodeEntered)
{
    numberCounter = 0;
```

```
        zipCounter = 0;
        foundNumber = "";
...
}
}
// Stop hiding the code here -->
</SCRIPT>
```

We have created two counter variables that we are going to use in `while` loops, and a third variable that we will use to store the outcome of our check.

Our next step is to create two `while` loops.

```
// Zip Code Check

zipCodeEntered =
document.forms['promotion'].elements['zipCode'].value;

if (zipCodeEntered)
{
        numberCounter = 0;
        zipCounter = 0;
        foundNumber = "";

        while (zipCounter < 5)
        {
            ...
            zipCounter++;
        }
}
...
}
// Stop hiding the code here -->
</SCRIPT>
```

The preceding script provides the basis for our first `while` loop. The script tells the engine to execute the statements that follow *while* the variable `zipCounter` is less than 5. At this point, there is only one statement that follows, but we will be adding to that in a moment. The statement that is there now, however, is the key to making sure we're not creating an infinite loop.

```
zipCounter++;
```

The preceding line takes the value of `zipCounter` and adds 1 to it, so that every time the loop is executed, `zipCounter` will have a value 1 higher than the previous pass until it reaches 5 and the condition is no longer met and the script can move on.

This first `while` loop will be used to cycle through all five characters in the zip code field. We will now add a second `while` loop within the first that we will use to cycle through all 10 digits (0–9).

```
// Zip Code Check

zipCodeEntered =
document.forms['promotion'].elements['zipCode'].value;

if (zipCodeEntered)
{
    numberCounter = 0;
    zipCounter = 0;
    foundNumber = "";

    while (zipCounter < 5)
    {
        while (numberCounter<10)
        {
            . . .
            numberCounter++;
        }
        if (foundNumber != "yes" )
        {
            zipCounter = 6;
        }
        else
        {
            zipCounter++;
            numberCounter = 0;
        }
    }
}
. . .
}
// Stop hiding the code here -->
</SCRIPT>
```

Now, the second `while` loop will test for the numbers 0–9 every time the first loop is run. For now, let's ignore the `if` statement at the end of the first loop and add the statements we need in the second loop.

```
// Zip Code Check

zipCodeEntered =
document.forms['promotion'].elements['zipCode'].value;
```

```
if (zipCodeEntered)
{
     numberCounter = 0;
     zipCounter = 0;
     foundNumber = "";

     while (zipCounter < 5)
     {
          while (numberCounter<10)
          {
               if (zipCodeEntered.substr(zipCounter, 1)
                  == numberCounter)
               {
                    foundNumber = "yes";
                    numberCounter = 11;
               }
               else
               {
                    foundNumber = "no";
               }
               numberCounter++;
          }
          if  (foundNumber != "yes" )
          {
               zipCounter = 6;
          }
          else
          {
               zipCounter++;
               numberCounter = 0;
          }
     }
}
...
}
// Stop hiding the code here -->
</SCRIPT>
```

In the preceding code, we added an if statement to the inside
of the second while loop. This if statement is the most important section of this part of the script—it is doing the actual testing
of the values in the zip code field, so let's go over it in more detail.
First, we are setting up the test of the value.

```
if (zipCodeEntered.substr(zipCounter, 1)   ==
numberCounter)
```

We are using the `substr()` method in this statement to test a specific character in the zip code field. When we used this method in Chapter 1, we specified a specific range of characters that we wanted to gather; in this example, we are only checking a single character and we are using the value of the variable `zipCounter` to tell the `substr()` method which character we want to check.

As the first loop cycles through, adding 1 to this variable each time it passes, we will be testing the characters that are at positions 0–4 of the `zipCodeEntered` variable. In other words, it will test all five characters of the zip code.

We will be comparing these values one at a time to the value of the variable `numberCounter`. This is the variable that is the basis for the evaluation of our second loop, and as the second loops cycles through its life, `numberCounter` is also having the value of 1 added to it each time. So, while the second loop is cycling, it is testing to see if the character located at the position of `zipCounter` is the same as the value of `numberCounter`, which is cycling through the digits 0–9.

If it is a match, the `if` statement will move on to set the variable `foundNumber` to `yes`, and it will set the value of `numberCounter` to 11 so that, on its next entry of the second `while` loop, the condition will be false and the script will move on. If it does not find a match it will set the value of `foundNumber` to `no`, add 1 to the value of `numberCounter`, and cycle through the second loop again searching for a match.

Once the second loop either runs through its 10 iterations or a match is found for a number, the script will continue on to the `if` statement we added to the first `while` loop earlier. This `if` statement tests the value of `foundNumber`. If in the second `while` loop a number is not found, it will set the `zipCounter` to 6, which will kick us out of the first `while` loop on the next pass and create an error message. If a number was found in the second loop, then the `if` statement will add 1 to the value of `zipCounter` and let it continue on to check the next character in the zip code field.

The final addition to this section of code will be to create another error message if a nonnumber was found in the zip code field.

```
// Zip Code Check

zipCodeEntered =
document.forms['promotion'].elements['zipCode'].value;
```

```
if (zipCodeEntered)
{
    numberCounter = 0;
    zipCounter = 0;
    foundNumber = "";

    while (zipCounter < 5)
    {
        while (numberCounter<10)
        {
            if (zipCodeEntered.substr(zipCounter, 1)
                == numberCounter)
            {
                foundNumber = "yes";
                numberCounter = 11;
            }
            else
            {
                foundNumber = "no";
            }
            numberCounter++;
        }
        if  (foundNumber != "yes" )
        {
            zipCounter = 6;
        }
        else
        {
            zipCounter++;
            numberCounter = 0;
        }
    }
    if (foundNumber != "yes")
    {
        zipCodeErrorMessage = "-zip code has non-numbers
        in it\r";
    }
}
...
}
// Stop hiding the code here -->
</SCRIPT>
```

In this section we have created some fairly difficult and advanced code. However, good news! We're almost finished! The only thing left to do is to check and see if any error messages were created and display them to the user or, if none were created, submit the form to the CGI script.

◆ Project III: Letting the User Know What's Wrong

This final piece of code is nothing groundbreaking—we will be using methods that we covered earlier in the chapter. If the world were a perfect place, then the user would have filled out the form properly. However, this isn't always the case, so now that we have gone through and made the necessary checks for missing or erroneous data, we need to pass on what we have found to the user. We will use a simple `if` statement to accomplish this.

```
// Letting the user know what was missed

if ((requiredFieldsErrorMessage) ||
    (whatTheyWantErrorMessage) || (emailErrorMessage) ||
    (areaCodeErrorMessage) || (zipCodeErrorMessage))
{
    . . .
}
else
{
    . . .
}
}
// Stop hiding the code here -->
</SCRIPT>
```

The first line checks to see if our error message variables have a value. If they do, that means that the user has missed something and we should compose a comprehensive error message for the user. We do this by first assigning the beginning of a message to the variable `alertMessage`, and then add any error messages created by our checks to the end.

```
// Letting the user know what was missed

if ((requiredFieldsErrorMessage) ||
    (whatTheyWantErrorMessage) || (emailErrorMessage) ||
    (areaCodeErrorMessage) || (zipCodeErrorMessage))
{
    alertMessage = "Oops! There's a little trouble with
    the information you've provided\r";

    //build remainder of the alert message
    alertMessage = alertMessage +
    requiredFieldsErrorMessage;
```

```
        alertMessage = alertMessage +
        whatTheyWantErrorMessage;

        alertMessage = alertMessage + emailErrorMessage;
        alertMessage = alertMessage + areaCodeErrorMessage;
        alertMessage = alertMessage + zipCodeErrorMessage;


        ...
    }
    else
    {
    ...
    }
    }
    // Stop hiding the code here -->
    </SCRIPT>
```

After we add any other error messages we have to the opening, all we need to do is use the `alert()` function to display our
completed message to the user.

```
    // Letting the user know what was missed

    if ((requiredFieldsErrorMessage) ||
        (whatTheyWantErrorMessage) || (emailErrorMessage) ||
        (areaCodeErrorMessage) || (zipCodeErrorMessage))
    {
        alertMessage = "Oops! There's a little trouble with
         the information you've provided\r";

        //build remainder of the alert message
        alertMessage = alertMessage +
        requiredFieldsErrorMessage;

        alertMessage = alertMessage +
        whatTheyWantErrorMessage;

        alertMessage = alertMessage + emailErrorMessage;
        alertMessage = alertMessage + areaCodeErrorMessage;
        alertMessage = alertMessage + zipCodeErrorMessage;

        alert (alertMessage);
    }
    else
    {
        ...
    }
    }
    // Stop hiding the code here -->
    </SCRIPT>
```

If there was nothing wrong with their answers, the `else` statement will go ahead and submit the form data to the CGI script.

```
// Letting the user know what was missed

if ((requiredFieldsErrorMessage) ||
    (whatTheyWantErrorMessage) || (emailErrorMessage) ||
    (areaCodeErrorMessage) || (zipCodeErrorMessage))
{
    alertMessage = "Oops! There's a little trouble with
    the information you've provided\r";

    //build remainder of the alert message
    alertMessage = alertMessage +
    requiredFieldsErrorMessage;

    alertMessage = alertMessage +
    whatTheyWantErrorMessage;

    alertMessage = alertMessage + emailErrorMessage;
    alertMessage = alertMessage + areaCodeErrorMessage;
    alertMessage = alertMessage + zipCodeErrorMessage;

    // Now, display the error message
    alert (alertMessage);
}
else
{
    document.forms['promotion'].submit();
}
}
// Stop hiding the code here -->
</SCRIPT>
```

REVIEWING THE SCRIPT

Well, if that isn't a mouthful, or should we say, a page full of JavaScript, then we don't know what is. On the upside, though, we now have a script that will have those marketing folks singing your praises to your boss. Let's look over the script one last time and review what we accomplished.

1. First, we created some variables that will hold the values the user has entered into the required fields, as well as variables to hold any error messages that need to be created.

```
<SCRIPT Language="JavaScript">
<!-- Code after this will be ignored by older browsers
```

```
//Create the errorCheck Function
function errorCheck()
{

        // Create some variables for our script
        var requiredFieldsErrorMessage = "";
        var firstNameEntered = "";
        var lastNameEntered = "";
        var emailEntered = "";
        var areaCodeEntered = "";
        var zipCodeEntered = "";
        var pullDownErrorMessage = "";
        var emailErrorMessage = "";
        var areaCodeErrorMessage = "";
        var zipCodeErrorMessage = "";
```

2. Next, we started to create the part of the function that will check for any omissions or errors in the user's answers and print out a message to let the user know what is wrong.

    The first step is to put the user's answers for the required fields into our new variables.

```
// Required fields error checking

firstNameEntered =
document.forms['promotion'].elements['firstName'].value;

lastNameEntered =
document.forms['promotion'].elements['lastName'].value;

emailEntered =
document.forms['promotion'].elements['email'].value;
```

3. Then, we set up a series of `if` statements to make sure that variables held data, and if not, to begin adding the omissions to the `requiredFieldsErrorMessage` variable.

```
if ((!firstNameEntered) || (!lastNameEntered) ||
    (!emailEntered))
{

    if (!firstNameEntered)
    {
        requiredFieldsErrorMessage = "- your first
        name\r";
    }
```

```
     if (!lastNameEntered)
     {
         requiredFieldsErrorMessage =
         requiredFieldsErrorMessage + "- your last
         name\r";
     }
     if (!emailEntered)
     {
         requiredFieldsErrorMessage =
         requiredFieldsErrorMessage + "- your email
         address\r";
     }
}
```

4. We then set up an `if` statement to make sure the user selected an option other than the default from the required pull-down menu. If the user didn't select another option, the script assigns a short message to the variable `pullDownErrorMessage`.

```
//Checking for pull-down errors
if (document.forms['promotion'].elements['whatTheyWant']
.value == 'default')
{
    pullDownErrorMessage = "- you didn't tell us what
    you want to see in Stitch";
}
```

5. The next step in our `errorCheck()` function was to set up a series of `if` statements that would look at the string entered in the e-mail form field and check for the presence of an @ symbol and a period.

```
// email error checking

if (emailEntered)
{
    emailEntered = document.forms['promotion']
    .elements['email'].value;

    emailValue = new String (emailEntered);
    emailHasAt = emailValue.indexOf("@");
    emailHasPeriod = emailValue.indexOf(".");

    if ((emailHasAt == -1) || (emailHasPeriod == -1))
    {
        emailErrorMessage = "-your email address\r";
    }
}
```

6. If the user entered a phone number, we needed to be sure that an area code for that number was also entered. Therefore, we set up another series of `if` statements that tested the values held in both of the form fields.

```
// Area Code Check

areaCodeEntered =
document.forms['promotion'].elements['areaCode'].value;

phoneNumber1Entered =
document.forms['promotion'].elements['phoneNumber1'].value;

if ((!areaCodeEntered) && (phoneNumber1Entered))
{
    areaCodeErrorMessage = "-please enter your area
    code\r";
}
```

7. Then, we checked to make sure that the zip code field contained only numbers. We set up `if` statements and two `while` loops to look at the individual characters of the string that was entered in the zip code field and test them to make sure they were integers.

```
// Zip Code Check

zipCodeEntered =
document.forms['promotion'].elements['zipCode'].value;

// we don't want to do anything if the visitor hasn't
// entered in anything for the zip code

if (zipCodeEntered)
{
    numberCounter = 0;
    zipLength =    5;
    zipCounter = 0;
    foundNumber = "";

    while (zipCounter < 5)
    {
        while (numberCounter<10)
        {
            if (zipCodeEntered.substr(zipCounter, 1)
                == numberCounter)
            {
                foundNumber = "yes";
                numberCounter = 11;
```

```
                    }
                    else
                    {
                          foundNumber = "no";
                    }
                    numberCounter++;
              }
              if  (foundNumber != "yes" )
              {
                    zipCounter = 6;
              }
              else
              {
                    zipCounter++;
                    numberCounter = 0;
              }
        }
        if (foundNumber != "yes")
        {
              zipCodeErrorMessage = "-zip code has non-numbers
              in it\r";
        }
  }
```

8. Finally, we set up some `if` statements to look at the values of the various error message variables. If they held a value, we added that value to the `alertMessage` variable. Once all of the error messages were tested, we printed out the content of the final message for the user to see. If no error messages were found, we called the `submit()` function of the form.

```
// Letting the user know what was missed

if ((requiredFieldsErrorMessage) ||
    (pullDownErrorMessage) || (emailErrorMessage) ||
    (areaCodeErrorMessage) || (zipCodeErrorMessage))
{
    alertMessage = "Oops! There's a little trouble with
    the information you've provided\r";

    //build remainder of the alert message
    alertMessage = alertMessage +
    requiredFieldsErrorMessage;

    alertMessage = alertMessage + pullDownErrorMessage;
    alertMessage = alertMessage + emailErrorMessage;
    alertMessage = alertMessage + areaCodeErrorMessage;
    alertMessage = alertMessage + zipCodeErrorMessage;
```

```
        // Now, display the error message
        alert ( alertMessage )
}
else // there are no problems with the form
{
        // send this form data to its CGI
        //document.forms['promotion'].submit()
}
}
</SCRIPT>
```

We have learned some new concepts in this chapter, and enhanced our knowledge of concepts that we have already discussed. Let's take a look at what we covered:

- The JavaScript hierarchy and our ability to access and manipulate its objects (especially form objects).
- If statements and while loops.
- The use of the alert() method as a means of delivering information to the user.
- Logical operators: ||, &&, and !.
- Entering a hard line break using \r.
- The STRING object and some of its properties.

RECAP

We covered a lot of ground in this chapter. If you can wrap your mind around these concepts and structures, then you're well on your way to mastering JavaScript. Understanding and using if statements and while loops is key to advanced JavaScript solutions—as you continue to use JavaScript this will become more apparent.

ADVANCED PROJECTS

Here are a few ideas that you can implement if you wish to further your understanding of the concepts covered in this chapter:

1. Try validating different form fields that weren't covered in this chapter, such as radio buttons.

2. Check text boxes for specific answers, possibly as a means to grade an online test.

5 JavaScript Windows and Frames

IN THIS CHAPTER

- A Look at the WINDOW Object
- Project I: Creating, Populating, and Closing Windows
- Project II: Using JavaScript to Talk Between Frames
- Recap
- Advanced Projects

Our newfound JavaScript knowledge has enabled us to do some pretty cool stuff. We've spent the last couple of chapters working with forms, and now it's time to move on to something new. Except for the homepage, the Stitch site is created using frames. In this chapter, we are going to work on some of the Stitch secondary pages and bring you up to speed on how JavaScript handles frames and windows.

Before we get into any specific projects, however, we are going to take a closer look at what windows and frames are and how they fall into Java-Script's object hierarchy. Dealing with frames and multiple windows can get quite complex and often times seem very convoluted. By the end of this chapter, we hope that you will have a solid understanding of how windows and frames, when combined with JavaScript, can help you do some great things.

117

◆ A Look at the WINDOW Object

The WINDOW object in JavaScript is on the top of the JavaScript hierarchy; the DOCUMENT object and the objects below it are all descendants of the WINDOW object. The projects that we have completed thus far have been contained within a single window, so we never had to deal with the WINDOW object or its properties. However, this will not always be the case. There are many occasions when it is advantageous to create a new window or access objects contained within another window.

Because the window is an object, we are able to access the properties and objects that it contains, as well as its own properties. Using JavaScript, we are able to modify a window's size, configure its toolbars, access its HISTORY array, and much more. Let's get into our first project and see what all this means.

◆ Project I: Creating, Populating, and Closing Windows

There's a page on the *Stitch* Web site that lists the companies that have placed ads in the current issue of the magazine. *Stitch* is *the* fashion magazine and it attracts some huge companies as advertisers—the ads themselves are often as groundbreaking as the fashion. Because the magazine is bombarded with requests from readers who want to get in touch with the companies, the powers that be think putting the ads on the Web site is a great idea. Therefore, they have decided to expand the functionality of the page and make each company's name a link that will take the user to a page with the company's contact information, a link to their Web site, and a link to a copy of their current ad.

Guess who they have come to with the job of making this a reality? That's right—you. No reason to fear, though. With your recent additions to the site you are beginning to be known as the office JavaScript guru. After a quick planning meeting with your boss, you think you have devised a great way to accomplish the task. The one problem that kept coming up was the fact that there will be at least 20 advertisers in each month's issue—this many pages added to the site will crowd the server and make for quite a few files to update each month. So, here's the plan: We're going to use JavaScript arrays on the existing list page to store all of the information we will need to dynamically create a page for each company, which we will then put into a new window. This will save space on the server, allow us to update one file a month, and give us one heck of a project for this chapter. There are three parts to creating this script: First, we will define and create the arrays for each company's information. Next, we will write the function that will open up our new window and populate it with the content. Finally, we will need to insert the proper event handlers into the HTML to make it all happen.

Creating and Defining the Arrays

The first thing we need to do is to create the arrays to hold the company information. We will to need to store nine items for each company: the company's name, street address, city, state, zip code, phone number, fax number, Web site (if it has one), and, finally, the URL for the page with the company's ad on it. In Chapter 3, we used two arrays for each group—one to hold the name of the page and the other to hold the location of the URL. For the most part, we are going to use the same idea here to store our company information; however, instead of two arrays for each group we will be using only one for each company. Whereas previously we assigned and referenced each element in the array by its position, in this project we are going to give each element a name that we can use to reference it.

Let's start the script by defining the arrays for the companies. Since this page isn't going to be added until the next issue, we don't know which companies will be placing ads. In the meantime, we will just create arrays for two fictitious companies, which will allow us to get our scripts working right away.

```
<SCRIPT Language="JavaScript">
<!-- Code after this will be ignored by older browsers

// Arrays for Company Information
    // Define the arrays

Company1_info = new Array(9);
Company2_info = new Array(9);
...

// Stop hiding the code here -->
</SCRIPT>
```

We have defined two arrays, one for Company1 and the other for Company2, and given each a length of nine elements. Next, we need to assign each company's contact information to the arrays. Let's put the information for Company1 into its array.

```
<SCRIPT Language="JavaScript">
<!-- Code after this will be ignored by older browsers

// Arrays for Company Information
    // Define the arrays

Company1_info = new Array(9);
Company2_info = new Array(9);

// Populate company1's array

Company1_info['name'] = 'Company 1';
Company1_info['street'] = '1235 company way #1';
Company1_info['city'] = 'Smallsville';
Company1_info['state'] = 'California';
Company1_info['zip'] = '91367';
Company1_info['phone'] = '818-555-1212';
Company1_info['fax'] = '818-555-1213';
Company1_info['website'] = 'http://www.company1.com';
Company1_info['ads'] = 'company1_ads.html';

// Stop hiding the code here -->
</SCRIPT>
```

When you are populating an array with as many elements as we are in the preceding code, it is often easier to assign each element a name instead of using its numeric position. It is easy to forget where a specific element is located if you are only using its position number as a reference.

The Company1_info array now holds all of the information we need to create a page for Company1 later in the script. Let's fill in the array for Company2.

```
<SCRIPT Language="JavaScript">
<!-- Code after this will be ignored by older browsers

// Arrays for Company Information
    // Define the arrays

Company1_info = new Array(9);
Company2_info = new Array(9);
```

```
// Populate company1's array

Company1_info['name'] = 'Company 1';
Company1_info['street'] = '1235 company way #1';
Company1_info['city'] = 'Smallsville';
Company1_info['state'] = 'California';
Company1_info['zip'] = '91367';
Company1_info['phone'] = '818-555-1212';
Company1_info['fax'] = '818-555-1213';
Company1_info['website'] = 'http://www.company1.com';
Company1_info['ads'] = 'company1_ads.html';

// Populate company2's array

Company2_info['name'] = 'Company 2';
Company2_info['street'] = '4321 company way #2';
Company2_info['city'] = 'Bigsville';
Company2_info['state'] = 'California';
Company2_info['zip'] = '91235';
Company2_info['phone'] = '818-555-2121';
Company2_info['fax'] = '818-555-2122';
Company2_info['website'] = 'http://www.company2.com';
Company2_info['ads'] = 'company2_ads.html';

// Stop hiding the code here -->
</SCRIPT>
```

We now have all the information we need stored safely in our two arrays (if you need a refresher on the basics of arrays, check out Project II in Chapter 3). It's time to move on to the next step.

Creating the Function

The function for this script is going to need to do several things. First, it will need to decide which company was chosen and gather its information from the proper array. Next, it needs to open a new window, and finally, we need to have it populate the new window with the information from the array. Let's first set up the framework for our function.

```
// Page Creator Function

function PageCreator(selection)
{
    ...
}

// Stop hiding the code here -->
</SCRIPT>
```

In the preceding code, we created the `PageCreator()` function and set up the variable `selection` to accept the value being passed to the function from the event handler. This value will be the name of the company that was chosen by the user. The next step is to find out which company the user chose and gather its information.

```
// Page Creator Function

function PageCreator(selection)
{

var company = eval(selection + "_info['name']");
var street = eval(selection + "_info['street']");
var city = eval(selection + "_info['city']");
var state = eval(selection + "_info['state']");
var zip = eval(selection + "_info['zip']");
var phone = eval(selection + "_info['phone']");
var fax = eval(selection + "_info['fax']");
var website = eval(selection + "_info['website']");
var ads = eval(selection + "_info['ads']");


. . .
}

// Stop hiding the code here -->
</SCRIPT>
```

Now we know that the value of `selection` is going to be the name of the company, and we have used those names in the names of the arrays that store their information. In the preceding code, we are using the `eval()` function to combine the variable value with a string, which, when combined, will call the information from the proper position of that company's array. After the information has been retrieved from the array it is then put into a variable that we will use later when printing the content of the pop-up window. This process is repeated for each of the nine different pieces of information that we are going to need.

Once we have the information for the selected company stored safely in our variables, we need to open up a new window in which to put that information. Let's have a quick look at the syntax of the `open()` method of the WINDOW object.

```
window.open(URL, windowName, windowFeatures)
```

There are three elements that you need to include within the open() method: the URL of the page that you want to put into the new window; a string that contains the name that you want the window to use when it is being referenced as a target in the <A HREF>; and an optional list of standard window properties that you can customize, such as width, height, or the inclusion of various toolbars.

A window is not only able to carry the name that will be used as a target, but it can also be associated with a name that you can use when referencing the WINDOW object using JavaScript. To assign it this second name you use the following syntax, where Name is the name you wish to assign to the window.

```
Name = window.open(URL, windowName, windowFeatures)
```

Let's put in the code that will open up the window in our script.

```
// Page Creator Function

function PageCreator(selection)
{

var company = eval(selection + "_info['name']");
var street = eval(selection + "_info['street']");
var city = eval(selection + "_info['city']");
var state = eval(selection + "_info['state']");
var zip = eval(selection + "_info['zip']");
var phone = eval(selection + "_info['phone']");
var fax = eval(selection + "_info['fax']");
var website = eval(selection + "_info['website']");
var ads = eval(selection + "_info['ads']");

// Open the new Window
infowin =
window.open("blank.html","Company_Info","menubar=yes,
width=250,height=200");


...
}

// Stop hiding the code here -->
</SCRIPT>
```

The first thing we are doing in the preceding code is assigning the new window the name `infowin`. Once that is done, we move on to the `open()` method itself—the URL of the page we want to put in the window is `blank.html`. We are going to be populating the window dynamically with content from our arrays, so that HTML page is as blank as its name suggests. The next element of the code is the target name we are assigning it—`Company_Info`. We won't be using this in our script but it is a required element. The next element is the list of attributes that we want the window to take on. We will be including the tool bar that contains the menus such as file, edit, view, and so forth, and we are giving the window a width of 250 pixels and a height of 200 pixels.

Now that we have opened our new window, we need to populate it with the information stored in our variables. To do this we are going to use the `document.write()` method. We have already used this method on several occasions in this book, but now we are going to add a new twist. If we were to use the standard syntax

```
document.write('text to be written');
```

we would simply be rewriting the content on our company listing page and not in our new window. To write to our new window we have to tell the JavaScript engine specifically where we want to write out our HTML. This can be accomplished by inserting the name of the window before `document`, as follows:

```
infowin.document.write('text to be written');
```

Now that we know how to write to our new window, let's add the code that will do just that.

```
// Page Creator Function

function PageCreator(selection)
{
    var company = eval(selection + "_info['name']");
    var street = eval(selection + "_info['street']");
    var city = eval(selection + "_info['city']");
    var state = eval(selection + "_info['state']");
    var zip = eval(selection + "_info['zip']");
```

```
var phone = eval(selection + "_info['phone']");
var fax = eval(selection + "_info['fax']");
var website = eval(selection + "_info['website']");
var ads = eval(selection + "_info['ads']");

// Open the new Window
infowin = window.open("blank.html","Company_Info",
"menubar=yes,width=250,height=200");

// Write content to new window
infowin.document.write
("<HTML><HEAD><TITLE>Company Information</TITLE>
  </HEAD><BODY BGCOLOR='#FFFFFF'><CENTER>")

infowin.document.write
("<TABLE BORDER='0'' CELLSPACING='0'
   CELLPADDING='0'><TR><TD><B>" + company + "</B>
  </TD></TR>");

infowin.document.write
("<TR><TD>" + street + "</TD></TR>");

infowin.document.write
("<TR><TD>" + city + ", " + state + "  " + zip +
 "</TD></TR>");

infowin.document.write
("<TR><TD>" + "phone - " + phone + "</TD></TR>
  <TR><TD>fax - " + fax + "</TD></TR>");

infowin.document.write
("<TR><TD><A HREF='" + website + "' TARGET='_TOP'>"
 + website + "</A></TD></TR>");

infowin.document.write
("<TR><TD ALIGN='CENTER'><BR><A HREF='" + ads +
 "' TARGET='Content'>View the Ad</A></TD></TR>
  </TABLE>");

infowin.document.write
("<TABLE BORDER='0'' CELLSPACING='0'
   CELLPADDING='0' WIDTH='249'><TR><TD WIDTH='249'
   VALIGN='BOTTOM' ALIGN='RIGHT'><BR>
  <A HREF='javascript:window.close()'><IMG
   SRC='images/closer.gif' BORDER='0'></A></TD>
  </TR>");

infowin.document.write
("<TR><TD WIDTH='249' BGCOLOR='#FFFF00'> </TD>
  </TR></TABLE>");
```

```
}

// Stop hiding the code here -->
</SCRIPT>
```

Let's look at what's going on in the preceding block of code. While it may seem like a lot, it really isn't. For the sake of legibility we are using multiple `document.write();` methods to write out our new code. In the first line, we are creating a new HTML document and inserting the HEAD and BODY tags. In previous scripts with `document.write()`, we used a backward slash (\) to escape quotes that we wanted to print out; in this example, we are simply using two types of quotes. We are using double quotes to signify the beginning and the end of the content we want printed, while inside those quotes we are using single quotes when we want them to actually be printed out in our code. Both this method and the \ method work equally well; which one you use is a matter of personal preference.

In the rest of the `document.write` lines we are using a combination of a table template and the information we have stored in our variables to print out as content. The second-to-last `document.write` line contains some unfamiliar scripting, so let's take a closer look at it.

For the most part, the content we are printing is pretty straightforward; however, if you look closely, you will see something new.

```
<A HREF='javascript:window.close()'>
```

The JavaScript link in this HREF can be thought of as an `onClick()` event handler—when the user clicks on the link, the JavaScript that follows the colon will be executed. In this case, the command will allow the user to close the new window once he or she has the necessary information from the page. Closing windows isn't something we've covered yet, so let's look at the `close()` method's syntax.

```
window.close();
```

By default, this line will close the window in which the information is found. If your goal was to close another browser window you would simply call its name specifically, as follows:

```
infowin.close()
```

The `document.write()` lines are the last part of our function. The only thing left to do in this script is to insert the event handlers into the HTML, and we will be off and running.

Inserting the Event Handlers

As in the `close()` method used previously in the pop-up window content, we are going to be putting our event handlers directly into the HREF tags of the HTML. When the user clicks on a company link, the `PageCreator()` function will be called and passed the name of that company (see Figure 5–1). The following HTML contains the links with the handlers inserted into the   HREF tags:

```
<TR>
    <TD>
             
    </TD>
    <TD>
        <FONT FACE="Helvetica, Arial" SIZE="-1">
        <A HREF="JavaScript:PageCreator('Company1')">
        Company 1</A></FONT>
    </TD>
    <TD>
        <FONT FACE="Helvetica, Arial" SIZE="-1">
        <A HREF="JavaScript:PageCreator('Company2')">
        Company 2</A></FONT>
    </TD>
</TR>
```

That about wraps it up for this project. Let's review what we did and look at the script as a whole.

REVIEWING THE SCRIPT

1. First, we defined and populated the arrays that would hold the information for each company's contact information.

   Instead of using the position in the array that the information would hold, we assigned a name to the location. This method enabled us to refer to the name instead of the numeric position.

```
<SCRIPT Language="JavaScript">
<!-- Code after this will be ignored by older browsers

// Arrays for Company Information
    // Define the arrays

Company1_info = new Array(9);
Company2_info = new Array(9);
```

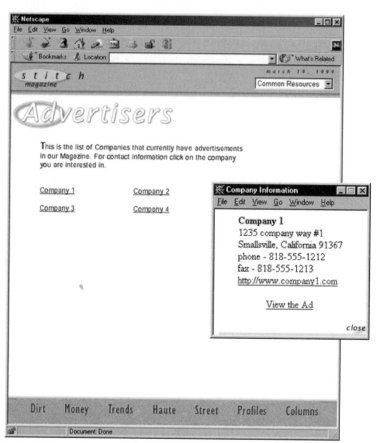

FIGURE 5–1 The advertisers index page

```
// Populate company1's array

Company1_info['name'] = 'Company 1';
Company1_info['street'] = '1235 company way #1';
Company1_info['city'] = 'Smallsville';
Company1_info['state'] = 'California';
Company1_info['zip'] = '91367';
Company1_info['phone'] = '818-555-1212';
Company1_info['fax'] = '818-555-1213';
Company1_info['website'] = 'http://www.company1.com';
Company1_info['ads'] = 'company1_ads.html';

// Populate company2's array
```

```
Company2_info['name'] = 'Company 2';
Company2_info['street'] = '4321 company way #2';
Company2_info['city'] = 'Bigsville';
Company2_info['state'] = 'California';
Company2_info['zip'] = '91235';
Company2_info['phone'] = '818-555-2121';
Company2_info['fax'] = '818-555-2122';
Company2_info['website'] = 'http://www.company2.com';
Company2_info['ads'] = 'company2_ads.html';
```

2. Our next step was to create the `PageCreator()` function.

We set up some variables to hold the company's information and use the value passed into the function from the event handlers to call the information out of the proper array.

```
// Page Creator Function

    function PageCreator(selection)
{
    var company = eval(selection + "_info['name']");
    var street = eval(selection + "_info['street']");
    var city = eval(selection + "_info['city']");
    var state = eval(selection + "_info['state']");
    var zip = eval(selection + "_info['zip']");
    var phone = eval(selection + "_info['phone']");
    var fax = eval(selection + "_info['fax']");
    var website = eval(selection + "_info['website']");
    var ads = eval(selection + "_info['ads']");
```

3. Once we put in the code to get the information out of the array, we used the `open()` method of the WINDOW object to create a new window to hold the company's information.

```
infowin=window.open("blank.html","Company_Info",
"menubar=yes,width=250,height=200");
```

4. With the new window created, we then used the `write()` method of the DOCUMENT object to print out our new content.

```
    infowin.document.write
    ("<HTML><HEAD><TITLE>Company Information</TITLE>
      </HEAD><BODY BGCOLOR='#FFFFFF'><CENTER>")

    infowin.document.write
    ("<TABLE BORDER='0'' CELLSPACING='0' CELLPADDING='0'>
    <TR><TD><B>" + company + "</B></TD></TR>");

    infowin.document.write
    ("<TR><TD>" + street + "</TD></TR>");
```

```
infowin.document.write
("<TR><TD>" + city + ", " + state + "  "  + zip +
 "</TD></TR>");

infowin.document.write
("<TR><TD>" + "phone - " + phone + "</TD></TR>
  <TR><TD>fax - " + fax + "</TD></TR>");

infowin.document.write
("<TR><TD><A HREF='" + website + "' TARGET='_TOP'>"
 + website + "</A></TD></TR>");

infowin.document.write
("<TR><TD ALIGN='CENTER'><BR><A HREF='" + ads +
 "' TARGET='Content'>View the Ad</A></TD></TR>
 </TABLE>");

infowin.document.write
("<TABLE BORDER='0'' CELLSPACING='0'
   CELLPADDING='0' WIDTH='249'><TR><TD WIDTH='249'
   VALIGN='BOTTOM' ALIGN='RIGHT'><BR>
   <A HREF='javascript:window.close()'>
   <IMG SRC='images/closer.gif' BORDER='0'></A>
   </TD></TR>");

infowin.document.write
("<TR><TD WIDTH='249' BGCOLOR='#FFFF00'> 
   </TD></TR></TABLE>");
}

// Stop hiding the code here -->
</SCRIPT>
```

5. The final step was to insert the event handlers into the
   <A HREF> tags of each company.

```
<TR>
    <TD>
             
    </TD>
    <TD>
        <FONT FACE="Helvetica, Arial" SIZE="-1">
        <A HREF="JavaScript:PageCreator('Company1')">
        Company 1</A></FONT>
    </TD>
    <TD>
        <FONT FACE="Helvetica, Arial" SIZE="-1">
        <A HREF="JavaScript:PageCreator('Company2')">
        Company 2</A></FONT>
```

```
    </TD>
</TR>
```

In writing this script we have used some features of JavaScript that are new to us. Let's take a look at them:

- The `WINDOW` object—we covered how to open, close, and populate windows.
- Populating and accessing array information by the numeric position that the information occupied and by user-defined labels.

We now have a clean and efficient way of dealing with what otherwise could have been a pretty tedious job. One of the great things about JavaScript is that it gives you the power to come up with solutions like this, which not only help handle the workload but are really cool uses of the technology.

Uh-oh, here comes the boss with another project for you. What do you say we check out what you're going to be tackling next?

◆ Project II: Using JavaScript to Talk Between Frames

Sure enough, there's a new issue that the boss wants you to look at on the Web site. Currently, on the bottom frame of the site that holds the main navigation, the graphics for the section you are in are high-lighted (see Figure 5–2). One of the other programmers has written the JavaScript to take care of changing the images when they are clicked on, but your boss needs you to take care of another problem.

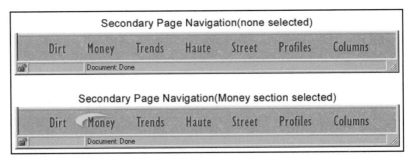

FIGURE 5–2 A *Stitch* secondary page's bottom navigation bar

If the user uses the Forward or Back buttons instead of actually clicking on the navigation images, the graphics won't update. Therefore, what we need to do is set up a script that will have the content frame talk to the navigation frame, so that when a new page is loaded into the content frame it will tell the navigation frame what graphic should be highlighted. For this project, we are going to need a little more information on how JavaScript handles frames.

Figuring Out Your Frame Hierarchy

A frame can be thought of as a sub-WINDOW object; like a window, it contains a DOCUMENT object as well as all of the descendant objects and properties that the HTML may create. If you look at the JavaScript hierarchy, however, you will see that the FRAME object sits below the WINDOW object; in fact, it is a property of the WINDOW object.

Each frame in a window can hold separate URLs. That ability can be very useful for our *Stitch* site, which uses three frames—one to hold content and two others to hold navigation. This lets the user scroll in the content frame while always leaving the navigation in place.

When an HTML document with a FRAMESET is loaded into the browser, the JavaScript engine creates an array that holds all of the FRAME objects being made. This is very similar to the way in which JavaScript handles the images that it finds on a page. How we go about referencing the objects is similar as well. Let's take a look at the FRAMESET for the *Stitch* site and see how we can reference the various FRAME objects that are created.

```
<FRAMESET ROWS="65,*,50" FRAMEBORDER="0" BORDER="0"
FRAMESPACING="NO">

    <FRAME NAME="Top_Nav_Bar" SRC="top_nav.html"
    MARGINWIDTH="0" MARGINHEIGHT="0" SCROLLING="no"
    FRAMEBORDER="no" NORESIZE>

    <FRAME NAME="Content" SRC="ad_index.html"
    MARGINWIDTH="0" MARGINHEIGHT="0" SCROLLING="auto"
    FRAMEBORDER="no" NORESIZE>

    <FRAME NAME="Bottom_Nav_Bar" SRC="bottom_nav.html"
    MARGINWIDTH="0" MARGINHEIGHT="0" SCROLLING="no"
    FRAMEBORDER="no" NORESIZE>

</FRAMESET>
```

The preceding code is the HTML that makes up the FRAMESET document. There are three frames that are called into existence within the FRAMESET: Top_Nav_Bar, which holds the common navigation and the header logo; Content, which holds all of the content for the sections of the site; and Bottom_Nav_Bar, which holds that navigation for the main sections of the site. Figure 5–3 illustrates this FRAMESET's hierarchy.

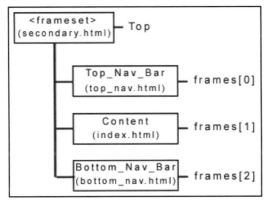

FIGURE 5–3 Our FRAME hierarchy

As the FRAMESET page is loaded, the frames are put into the FRAMES array in the order in which they are read by the engine: Top_Nav_Bar is frames[0], Content frame is frames[1], and Bottom_Nav_Bar is frames[2]. To access the FRAME objects, we use these position numbers when calling the FRAMES array. For example, if we wanted to access the URL of the Content frame, the syntax would look like this:

```
frames[1].src
```

However, this will work only if you are requesting the information from the page holding the FRAMESET. If we were in one of the other frames, we would have to tell the JavaScript engine to first go back to the top level of the window and then go to the Content frame. There are two ways to do this: You could use the line

```
top.frames[1].src
```

to tell the engine to go to the very top level of the hierarchy and then move on to the second frame in the FRAMES array. You could also use parent instead of top to achieve the same effect:

```
parent.frames[1].src
```

The difference is that `top` sends the engine to the top of the hierarchy, whereas `parent` only moves the pointer up one level to the object that is the parent of the frame from which you are calling. There will be times when you run into nested frames; in other words, the HTML document that is called in a frame contains another FRAMESET instead of just HTML. This will add another set of layers to the hierarchy, so to get to the top of the hierarchy you would need to use `parent` multiple times:

```
parent.parent.frames[1].src
```

Working with nested frames in JavaScript can get rather convoluted—luckily, the *Stitch* site contains no nested frames. With that said, let's get on with our project.

This project consist of two sections: First, we need to create a function in the `Bottom_Nav_Bar` that will change the highlighted graphic when the `Content` page changes. Second, we need to insert event handlers into all of the pages that populate the `Content` frame, which will call the function that we create in the first part of the project.

Creating a Function to Check Which Section You're In

Before we get into writing our new function, it will be very helpful to take a look at the existing function—it stands to reason that we may be able to use this function in our script. This function does two jobs: First, when it is called after the user has clicked on one of the Navigation images, it goes through and turns all of the Navigation images to the `Off` state. Once it has done that, it then goes and looks to see what graphic the user clicked on and turns that image to the `On` state. Let's look at the function itself so we can get an idea of how this is accomplished.

```
function Highlighter(current)
{
    var test = 1;
    while (test < 8)
    {
        document.images[test].src = eval("Pic"
        + test + "Off.src");

        ++ test;
    }
```

```
document.images[current].src = eval(current
+ "On.src");

able = current;
}
```

In the first line of the function, the variable `test` is being set to the value of 1—this value is going to be used as a test in the `while` loop that follows. The next line is the beginning of the `while` loop; as long as `test` is less than 8, the loop will keep cycling through. With `test` set to 1 when you enter the function, the loop will cycle seven times—once for each of the Navigation images. We are starting the value of `test` at 1 instead of 0 because the background image for the frame takes up the first position in the IMAGE array, and we need to skip over it when we are turning off the images.

Inside the loop we are changing the source of the image located at the same position as the value of `test` to the `off` version of the graphic. When the `while` loop finishes, all of the Navigation objects will have been turned to their default `Off` condition.

Now that all of the images are off, it's time to turn on the one the user has just clicked. The next line in the function takes care of this by setting the source of the image matching the value of the variable `current` to the rolled-over position.

The final line in the function sets the value of the variable `able` to the name of the category clicked on, which is held in the variable `current`. The variable `able` is used as a test in the `off()` function, one of the two functions that handles the roll-overs on the page.

```
function off(pic)
{
    if(document.images)
    {
        if (pic != able)
{
            document.images[pic].src= eval(pic
            + "Off.src");
        }
    }
}
```

Therefore, if you roll off the graphic of the section you are currently in, it won't turn off. We will be using this variable in our function as well.

Now that we have seen what's currently going on in the page, it's time to put in our function. Compared to the existing function, ours should be a walk in the park. Our new function is going to be called every time a new HTML page is loaded into the Content frame, but we only want it to change an image if the page that is loaded is from a different section than the previous page. To do this we will pass a value into the function when it is called; that value will be the name of the section that the page is in. Then, we are going to test that value against the value of the variable able, which contains the name of the section that the user last clicked on. We only want to run the rest of the function if those values are different; in other words, if the section has changed. With that said, let's get started with the function.

```
function SectionChecker(content)
{
     if (content != able)
     {
          . . .
     }
}
```

In the preceding code, we started the function and added the if statement that will test the value of content against that of able. Now, there is only one more addition needed to finish the function—inserting the code that we want executed if the values differ.

```
function SectionChecker(content)
{
     if (content != able)
     {
          Highlighter(content);
     }
}
```

Because the existing function already contains the Highlighter() function that will turn off all seven graphics and then turn on the one with the name that we pass into the function, all we have to do is call that function and pass it the value that was given to our function by the content page.

As a result, if the page that is loaded into the Content frame passes the value dirt into our function, then our function will call the Highlighter() function and pass along that same value, which will, in essence, turn off all of the Navigation images except for the dirt image. Now all we have to do is insert the event handlers into all of the pages that go into the Content frame.

Inserting the Event Handler

Until now, we have relied on event handlers that were reacting to some interaction with the user: rolling over an image, clicking a button, or changing some form field. For this project, however, what we need is a handler that will trigger when an HTML page is loaded by the browser. Well, it's our lucky day—the onLoad() handler does just that. All you need to do is place the onLoad() handler into the <BODY> tag of the HTML document. For our purposes, let's put it in one of the content pages for the Dirt section.

```
<BODY onLoad=". . . ">
```

Now that we've inserted the handler, let's put in the call to the SectionChecker() function. Remember that because the Section-Checker() function is located in another frame, we are going to have to specify the path to the function when calling it.

```
<BODY onLoad="top.frames[2].SectionChecker('dirt')">
```

Believe it or not, that's about it; you just need to put this handler in all of the HTML pages for the Content frame. The only element that will vary is the value that you are passing to the SectionChecker() function; that value will be the name of the section in which the page resides.

We're not done yet, though. One of the company's programmers was checking the new addition to the site and has found what could be a potential problem with the script. It's possible that the onLoad() handler could trigger before the Bottom_Nav_Bar frame containing the function is loaded. If this happens, it will generate a JavaScript error.

To prevent this from happening, we want to make sure that the Bottom_Nav_Bar frame is loaded before calling the Section-Checker() function from the Content frame. Therefore, we need to add some code to the FRAMESET page, the Bottom_Nav_Bar page, and all of the content pages. First, let's insert the needed code into the FRAMESET page. We know that if either the Content frame or the Bottom_Nav_Bar frame is loaded, the FRAMESET page itself must be loaded, so we will use a variable placed in the FRAMESET page to run our test.

```
<SCRIPT Language="JavaScript">
<!-- Code after this will be ignored by older browsers

var capable = 'no';
```

```
// Stop hiding the code here -->
</SCRIPT>
```

All we are doing in the preceding code is creating a variable called `capable` and assigning it the default value of `no`. When the `FRAMESET` page is loaded, the `capable` variable will be created for us. Next, let's put the code we need into the `Bottom_Nav_Bar` frame.

We need to insert a line of code that will call the `capable` variable in the `FRAMESET` page and assign it the value `yes`—you can put it in right after the `SectionChecker()` function.

```
function SectionChecker(content)
{
      if (content != able)
      {
            Highlighter(content);
      }
}

top.capable = 'yes';

// Stop hiding the code here -->
</SCRIPT>
```

Again, as with the `onLoad()` handler, we need to tell the browser how to get to `variable` in the hierarchy. When the `Bottom_Nav_Bar` frame is loaded, it will now change the `capable` variable to hold the value `yes`.

The last bit of code we need to put in is in the content pages. Let's make the change to the same Dirt section page that we put the `onLoad()` handler in already. The first thing we need to do is change the `onLoad()` handler.

```
<BODY BGCOLOR="White" onLoad="Checker()">
```

Instead of calling the `SectionChecker()` frame directly as we did before, we are going to create a new function on the content page itself that will call the `SectionChecker()` function. This new `Checker()` function is the function that we are now going to be calling in the `onLoad()` event handler. Once we create the `Checker()` function, we'll be done.

```
<SCRIPT Language="JavaScript">
<!-- Code after this will be ignored by older browsers
```

```
function Checker()
{
    if (top.capable='yes')
    {
        top.frames[2].SectionChecker('dirt');
    }
}

// Stop hiding the code here -->
</SCRIPT>
```

This function is quite simple. The first thing that happens when it's called is that we use an `if` statement to test the value of the capable variable on the FRAMESET page. If the `Bottom_Nav_Bar` frame has been loaded, it will have changed the value of `capable` to `yes`, so we can call the `SectionChecker()` function. However, if the `Bottom_Nav_Bar` frame hasn't been loaded, nothing will happen.

Well, that's it. All you need to do is insert the `onLoad()` handler and the `Checker()` function into the other pages that are located in the `Content` frame. Then, you can use the Back and Forward buttons to your heart's content and always know what section you are in.

REVIEWING THE SCRIPT

Let's take a look at our script and how we built it.

1. First, we were able to incorporate the functionality of an existing script into this project.

```
function Highlighter(current)
{
    var test = 1;
    while (test < 8)
    {
        document.images[test].src = eval("Pic"
        + test + "Off.src");

        ++ test;
    }
    document.images[current].src = eval(current
    + "On.src");

    able = current;
}
```

2. Next, we added the `SectionChecker()` function to the page located in the `Bottom_Nav_Bar` frame. This will call the

`Highlighter()` function and pass it the name of the section in which the page loaded in to the `Content` frame belongs.

```
function SectionChecker(content)
{
    if (content != able)
    {
        Highlighter(content);
    }
}
```

3. Then, we inserted the `onLoad()` event handler into all of the HTML pages that will show up in the `Content` frame. Within the handler we put in a call to our `SectionChecker()` function and passed it the name of the section in which the page belongs.

```
<BODY onLoad="top.frames[2].SectionChecker('dirt')">
```

Once the event handlers were inserted, our script was functional; however, to make it a bit more robust we decided to add a final touch that would prevent us from getting errors if the `Bottom_Nav_Bar` frame hadn't loaded before the `Section-Checker()` function was called.

1. First, we added a variable to the HTML page that held the FRAMESET. We will use this variable to test whether or not the `Bottom_Nav_Bar` frame has been loaded.

```
<SCRIPT Language="JavaScript">
<!-- Code after this will be ignored by older browsers

var capable = 'no';

// Stop hiding the code here -->
</SCRIPT>
```

2. Next, we added a line of code to the HTML page in the `Bottom_Nav_Bar` frame that will change the value of the variable in the FRAMESET page to tell us that the bottom Navigation page has been loaded by the browser.

```
function SectionChecker(content)
{
    if (content != able)
    {
        Highlighter(content);
    }
}
```

```
top.capable = 'yes';

// Stop hiding the code here -->
</SCRIPT>
```

3. Finally, we added a function to all of the HTML that goes in the `Content` frame and modified the `onLoad()` handler to call this new function instead of calling our `SectionChecker()` function directly.

```
<SCRIPT Language="JavaScript">
<!-- Code after this will be ignored by older browsers

function Checker()
{
    if (top.capable='yes')
    {
        top.frames[2].SectionChecker('dirt');
    }
}

// Stop hiding the code here -->
</SCRIPT>

</HEAD>
<BODY BGCOLOR="White" onLoad="Checker()">
```

RECAP

Working with windows and frames can greatly increase the functionality of your Web site—when used in conjunction with Java-Script, the sky is the limit as to what you can accomplish. In this chapter, we have just scratched the surface of what you can do with these features.

The concept of frames and understanding how their hierarchy works is not an easy thing to grasp, but once you have the fundamentals down it will open up a vast range of new applications.

ADVANCED PROJECTS

1. Use the technique from the first project in this chapter in a site with nested frames, where you will have two sets of navigation images that need to be tracked—one for the main navigation and another for secondary navigation.

2. Create a frames-based site with a set of nested frames where you can hide the navigation frame by changing the location property of the frame that holds the inner frames.

6 Advanced JavaScript

IN THIS CHAPTER

- Project I: Create Submenus for the *Stitch* Secondary Pages
- Recap
- Advanced Projects

Now that you have the basics down, it's time to move on to some hard-core, complex crowd-pleasers, guaranteed to elicit rave reviews from clients and friends.

◆ Project I: Create Submenus for the *Stitch* Secondary Pages

Studies have shown that people tend to get lost in most Web sites—they simply have a hard time finding the information they're after. Studies have also shown that most people get on the Web to find specific information. "Who reads studies?" you ask. Well, your boss, of course. In fact, he wants you to come up with some concepts for souping up the navigation on the *Stitch* home-page. So, you're whisked off to a brainstorming meeting with the other programmers. When it's your turn to suggest an idea, you propose a system of graphical submenus—where users get to preview what's in a section before having to actually go there. Before the sentence is out of your mouth you see your boss's eyes light up: Guess what our next project is going to be? You got it—a new *Stitch* homepage with a JavaScript-enhanced submenu system.

Functional Specification

Since this is a little complicated, we're going to spell out exactly what we want to happen before we start coding. It's tempting to skip this step and just jump into the code, but control yourself. Thinking through the project before you start will always save you time and usually results in a better end product.

Figure 6–1 is a screenshot of the existing *Stitch* homepage. It already has a great design going for it, and a submenu system should work well within its present design.

Currently, we have the logo at the top with the header for the spring fashion season, and a short common resource menu underneath it on the right-hand side. The main navigation categories are off to the left and a small graphical blurb sits in the middle of the page. Finally, there's a picture of a woman sitting on a boat off to the far right and bottom of the page.

What we want to do is allow a user to roll over one of the main navigation options, and have another menu pop up and replace the graphical blurb. For example, if a user rolls over "Haute," we want a list of some of the articles in the Haute section to appear where the blurb exists. Then, the user should be able to navigate directly to that article, bypassing the main Haute page by clicking on one of the sublevel articles.

A new menu should appear each time a user rolls over the name of a main section of the site. For example, when the user rolls over "Street," a menu with a list of articles in the Street section appears. When the user rolls over "Profiles," a list of articles within the Profiles section appears.

Whenever the user rolls over another main section, that section's secondary menu replaces the menu that was already there. When none of the main navigation images are being rolled over, the graphical blurb will return.

And there's more: Once the secondary menu appears, the main navigation image the user has rolled over should be high-lighted in some way so the user knows which secondary menu he

FIGURE 6–1 The current *Stitch* homepage

or she is viewing. The user should also be able to roll over the individual items in the secondary menu, and they should be highlighted.

Let's start looking at some realities of the page. By introducing secondary navigation, we will not only change the image of the category the user rolls over, but we also need a whole new image that contains the secondary categories that appear (see Figure 6–2). Where is that image going to go? Fortunately, that's the easy part. As stated earlier, we'll be replacing the graphical text blurb located to the right of the main navigation.

Here are the different goals that we need our script to accomplish:

1. Identify which primary navigation category, (for example, "Dirt," "Street," and so forth) the user is rolling over.

FIGURE 6–2 Homepage showing the secondary navigation for the Dirt section

2. Highlight that primary navigation category with a rollover.

3. Replace the default text blurb with the appropriate secondary navigation submenu.

4. When the user rolls over the items on the secondary navigation, the individual choice being rolled over should be highlighted.

5. When the user rolls off the secondary submenu, we want the menu to disappear and be replaced by the default text blurb; and the main navigation category should be unhighlighted and returned to its default state.

There are two main ways in which we could break up the menu images: We can make a single image and use an image map to set the proper hot spots and replace the whole image each time a category is rolled over, or we can cut up the primary navigation images so that each is contained within its own graphic, and then replace the image that is currently being rolled over. For our purposes, the second method will work best. This means that there are two versions for each of the main navigation categories: normal and highlighted. It also means that there are several versions of each submenu. It has been decided by the powers that be that there should be four links on each submenu. As a result, there'll be five versions of that submenu image: one normal image and four with the various choices highlighted. Since each submenu image has four different choices on it, we will need to create an image map for it.

<PLUG TYPE="SHAMELESS">
This sort of submenus/navigation technique is about a million times easier in DHTML. If you want to learn more, check out the DHTML book in this series—*Essential CSS & DHTML for Web Professionals*. It assumes you already know some HTML and JavaScript, and would be a good read after you finish this book. Honest.
</PLUG>

For the *Stitch* site, there are seven different main navigation images—that's a total of 14 main navigation images (1 normal, 1 highlighted for each). At the top, we've decided to limit the submenus to four choices each, so each submenu needs five separate images. That adds up to a subtotal of 35 submenu images and a grand total of 49 images.

That's a lot of images to manage. This means you can build a gazillion if statements to keep track of everything, or you can build a system that keeps track of all the necessary information for you. To make our lives easy, let's choose the latter. And, since this is a magazine with changing content, it'd be nice to build some code that's easy to update with new links or even new sections.

You should also note that since this method involves a lot of images, it's wise to make sure those images have a very small file size or risk massive download time. We'll need to tell the designer to go for a minimalist look.

Creating and Populating the Arrays to Store Data

The first step in our project is to create two global variables: whichMenu to keep track of which main navigation category the user most recently rolled over, and which secondary submenu we need to display; and overImage to help us make sure we are turning off images only when necessary.

To keep track of all the images, we need to create a multi-dimensional array, which we'll call section. Until now, we have been exposed only to single-dimensional arrays; multidimensional arrays work in much the same way but give us expanded capabilities. If you think of a single-dimensional array as a filing cabinet and each of the entries in the array as a drawer that holds a single piece of information, then a multidimensional array would have several file folders in each of the cabinet drawers. This would make each drawer within the main filing cabinet a filing cabinet itself.

In our section array, the first dimension will be the seven main categories, which will each in turn hold the second dimension, which will store all of the individual choices for the categories' submenu. Here's how we'll build it; first we will define our two global variables:

```
<SCRIPT Language="JavaScript ">
<!-- Code after this will be ignored by older browsers

var whichMenu=" ";
var overImage = 'no'


    . . .


// Stop hiding the code here -->
</SCRIPT>
```

We have given both of these variables default values that will make more sense as we work further into the script. For now, let's move on to the creation of our array.

```
<SCRIPT Language="JavaScript ">
<!-- Code after this will be ignored by older browsers

var whichMenu=" ";
var overImage = 'no'
```

```
section = new Array(4);

    section['dirt'] = new Array (4)
        section['dirt'][0] = 'supermodel'
        section['dirt'][1] = 'affairnet'
        section['dirt'][2] = 'moss'
        section['dirt'][3] = 'married'

    section['money'] = new Array (4)
        section['money'][0] = 'worldclique'
        section['money'][1] = 'germany'
        section['money'][2] = 'mergers'
        section['money'][3] = 'nmearnings'

    section['trends'] = new Array (4)
        section['trends'][0] = 'tshirts'
        section['trends'][1] = 'sweatshirts'
        section['trends'][2] = 'hats'
        section['trends'][3] = 'mugs'

    section['haute'] = new Array (4)
        section['haute'][0] = 'paris'
        section['haute'][1] = 'gaudy'
        section['haute'][2] = 'taffeta'
        section['haute'][3] = 'royalty'

    section['street'] = new Array (4)
        section['street'][0] = 'angry'
        section['street'][1] = 'prison'
        section['street'][2] = 'skater'
        section['street'][3] = 'hip_hop'

    section['profiles'] = new Array (4)
        section['profiles'][0] = 'moxon'
        section['profiles'][1] = 'west'
        section['profiles'][2] = 'trinidaddy'
        section['profiles'][3] = 'spurn'

    section['columns'] = new Array (4)
        section['columns'][0] = 'column1'
        section['columns'][1] = 'column2'
        section['columns'][2] = 'column3'
        section['columns'][3] = 'column4'

...

// Stop hiding the code here -->
</SCRIPT>
```

Let's take a close look at what's happening in the preceding code. Here is the first line that we added:

```
section = new Array(4);
```

This line should look pretty familiar to you—we created arrays for the Advertisers section of the *Stitch* site using the same method. This line is telling the JavaScript runtime engine to create an array called `section` and give it a length of 4. The next line is where we are heading into new territory.

```
section['dirt'] = new Array (4)
```

This line creates a new array and inserts it into our `section` array at the position `dirt`—now we have the first step in our multidimensional array. We then filled the `dirt` array.

```
section['dirt'][0] = 'supermodel'
section['dirt'][1] = 'affairnet'
section['dirt'][2] = 'moss'
section['dirt'][3] = 'married'
```

Once we had set up the `dirt` array, the rest of the code was created and filled the arrays that will hold the information for the other six categories.

Let's look at the names that we assigned to the information contained in the CATEGORY arrays. These names have meaning and will be important later in the script. Until now, we have always created new IMAGE objects to hold the images that we would use for rollovers; for this project we are going to use another method. When replacing images in this script we are simply going to set the `source` property of the initial image to a new path, and the names that we have stored in the arrays are going to help us do that. For example, there's an article in the Dirt section entitled "Supermodel Diet," so when the user has the Dirt section highlighted and its submenu is up, one of the options on the submenu will be "Supermodel Diet." Now, if the user rolls over that option we must swap out the default submenu with one that has the Supermodel option highlighted. By naming that graphic `supermodel.gif` we can simply use the information stored in our arrays to create the name of the gif on the fly as we change the `source` property of the default submenu. This may seem slightly overwhelming at the moment, but it will all make sense soon.

Creating the Functions to Run the Submenu System

Now that we have our arrays created and populated, we have to create several functions to run our submenu system. Let's start with the function that will be called when we roll over one of the main navigation images.

```
function mainNavOn (sectionName)
{
     overImage='yes';

     // make sure user already rolled over a
     // main nav image
     if (whichMenu != " ")
     {
          . . .
     }
     . . .
}

// Stop hiding the code here -->
</SCRIPT>
```

There are many ways for the graphics on the homepage to be highlighted, and it is going to be important for us to always be able to tell when the user is over an image. The first line of code in our new function will help us keep track of this. Since this function is called only when the user is over one of the main navigation images, we are setting the variable `overImage` to a value of `yes`.

The next line in the code will help us turn off the image that the user just left. To do this we will use the `whichImage` variable that we declared at the top of our script. A little further on in our function we will be resetting this variable to contain the name of the section that the user has just rolled over. As we first come into our function, the `whichImage` variable is either going to contain the name of the last category the user rolled over; if the user hasn't rolled over anything yet, it will still hold the value that we assigned it at the beginning of the script. The next line of code in our script is an `if` statement that tells the JavaScript runtime engine to execute the next bit of code, as long as the value of `whichImage` doesn't contain its default value.

Let's add the code that is going to reside within the `if` statement and see just what it will do.

```
function mainNavOn (sectionName)
{
     overImage='yes';
```

```
// make sure user already rolled over a
// main nav image
if (whichMenu != " ")
{
    // unhighlight old section name
    eval ("document." + whichMenu + ".src =
    'images/nav/" + whichMenu + ".gif'");
}


    . . .

}


// Stop hiding the code here -->
</SCRIPT>
```

This new line of code is the first real example of how we will handle image replacements in this script. Using this method requires a certain amount of discipline, so a close look at what's going on will be helpful. For argument's sake, let's say the user rolled off the "Dirt" category; if this were the case, the variable whichImage would contain the value dirt. Let's see how our new line of code will read with this value.

```
document.dirt.src = 'images/nav/dirt.gif';
```

The preceding line will attempt to change the source property of the IMAGE object dirt to the dirt.gif image located in the images/nav/ directory. To make this method work, we will need all of the default unhighlighted versions of the main categories to be named using the following syntax:

```
"Name of the Category" + .gif
```

The highlighted versions of the graphics will also need to use the following syntax in their naming:

```
"Name of the Category" + _over.gif
```

You should now have a pretty good understanding of our new method for image replacement. This method is a good one to use if you have control of the naming convention used for the images. If you don't have that control, there is no way to guarantee they will be named properly, so it would be best to stick with the method we have been using.

Once the old image has been unhighlighted, we need to update our `whichMenu` variable to hold the name of the category that the user is currently over so that we can highlight the image.

```
function mainNavOn (sectionName)
{
     overImage='yes';

     // make sure user already rolled over a
     // main nav image
     if (whichMenu != " ")
     {
          // unhighlight old section name
          eval ("document." + whichMenu + ".src =
          'images/nav/" + whichMenu + ".gif'");
     }

     // set variable to new rollover
     whichMenu = sectionName;


     . . .
}

// Stop hiding the code here -->
</SCRIPT>
```

In this new line, we are setting `whichImage` to hold the value contained within `sectionName`, which is the name of the section the user has just rolled over. Once we have done this, we add more new code to change the image currently being rolled over to its highlighted version.

```
function mainNavOn (sectionName)
{
     overImage='yes';

     // make sure user already rolled over a
     // main nav image
     if (whichMenu != " ")
     {
          eval ("document." + whichMenu + ".src =
          'images/nav/" + whichMenu + ".gif'") ;
     }

     // set variable to new rollover
     whichMenu = sectionName;
```

```
        // highlight the new image
        eval( "document." + whichMenu + ".src = 'images/
        nav/" + whichMenu + "_over.gif'");


            . . .
    }


    // Stop hiding the code here -->
    </SCRIPT>
```

This new line should look very similar to the line we used to turn off the previously rolled-over image—the only difference is that we have added _over to the name of the gif. As long as we have followed the proper naming convention, the image that the user has rolled over should now be highlighted.

Finally, the last step in this function is to bring up the appropriate submenu image. When we first bring up the submenu, none of the secondary categories will be highlighted, so we will call the default version of the graphic.

```
    function mainNavOn (sectionName)
    {
        overImage='yes';

        // make sure user already rolled over a
        // main nav image
        if (whichMenu != " ")
        {
            eval ("document." + whichMenu + ".src =
            'images/nav/" + whichMenu + ".gif'");
        }

        // set variable to new rollover
        whichMenu = sectionName;

        // highlight the new image
        eval( "document." + whichMenu + ".src = 'images/
        nav/" + whichMenu + "_over.gif'");

        // bring up secondary navigation image
        eval("document.submenu.src = 'images/nav/" +
        whichMenu + "_sec_blank.gif'");


    }

    // Stop hiding the code here -->
    </SCRIPT>
```

All of the default submenu images must have the following naming syntax:

```
"Name of Category" + sec_blank.gif
```

We will cover the naming syntax for the highlighted versions of the submenu images in the submenuOn() function, which will take care of highlighting the proper submenu category.

Once again, the first step is to set the value of the variable overImage to yes so that the scripts know that the user is currently over an image.

```
function submenuOn (sectionNum)
{
        overImage='yes';


            . . .


}


// Stop hiding the code here -->
</SCRIPT>
```

Next, when someone rolls over the area that is image-mapped for the submenus, we want to make sure that one of the main navigation images has already been rolled over and a submenu is actually visible before we start highlighting individual items on the submenu. If the user just rolls over the text blurb, we don't want any of the submenus popping up. We can check to see if a submenu is already visible by looking at the value of the whichMenu variable. If the variable contains the name of a section instead of the default blank value, then we know one of the main categories has been rolled over and a secondary submenu is showing. We will test this using an if statement like the one at the beginning of our first function.

```
function submenuOn (sectionNum)
{
        overImage='yes';

        if (whichMenu != " ")
        {
                . . .
        }
}


// Stop hiding the code here -->
</SCRIPT>
```

In our `if` statement, we first need to determine which secondary category the user has rolled over on the submenu image. This is where our multidimensional array starts to come in handy.

```
function submenuOn (sectionNum)
{
        overImage='yes';

        if (whichMenu != " ")
        {
                // determine name of subsection
                // user is rolling over
                subSection = section[whichMenu][sectionNum];
                ...
        }
}

// Stop hiding the code here -->
</SCRIPT>
```

In the preceding code, we are using `whichMenu` to point to the location in the first level of the array that holds the nested array, which contains the information for the secondary categories of the main category that is currently selected. `sectionNum` contains a number value that corresponds to the position of the secondary category the user has rolled over.

If the user rolled over the "Supermodel Diet" secondary category of the Dirt section, the right-hand side of the equation would read as follows:

```
section['dirt'][0]
```

This in turn would call to that position in our array and return the value of `supermodel`, which is then put into the variable `subSection`.

Now that we have the proper secondary submenu category tucked away in a variable, our next step is to replace the submenu graphic with the one that has the proper category highlighted.

```
function submenuOn (sectionNum)
{
        overImage='yes';

        if (whichMenu != " ")
        {
                // determine name of subsection
                // user is rolling over
                subSection = section[whichMenu][sectionNum];
```

```
        // swap out appropriate image
        eval("document.submenu.src = 'images/nav/" +
        whichMenu + "_" + subSection + "_over.gif'");
    }
}

// Stop hiding the code here -->
</SCRIPT>
```

As with all of our other image replacements, we need to use a specific naming syntax. For our highlighted secondary categories, the syntax is as follows:

```
"Name of Main Category" + "name of secondary category"
 + "_over.gif"
```

We now have both of the functions that will turn on our various images. Next, we need to create the functions that will turn off highlighted images when the user rolls off them. Like our secondary page rollovers from Chapter 2, we will have to be kind of crafty here. We don't want a main navigation image turning off just because we rolled over the submenu, so we are going to use two different functions. Let's get going on the first one.

```
function mapOff ()
{
    if (whichMenu != " ")
    {
        . . .
    }
}

// Stop hiding the code here -->
</SCRIPT>
```

Once again, the first thing we have to do is make sure that up until this function is called, the user was indeed over a graphic; so we will set up an if statement to check the value of whichMenu. Once it has been determined that it is okay to proceed, the next step is to change the value of the variable overImage to no, as the user has rolled off an image, thereby calling this current function.

```
function mapOff ()
{
    if (whichMenu != " ")
    {
        overImage = 'no';
```

```
        . . .
    }
}

// Stop hiding the code here -->
</SCRIPT>
```

The final step is to put in the `setTimeout` method, which will wait for a couple of seconds and then call the second function we will need to turn off the highlighted images.

```
function mapOff ()
{
    if (whichMenu != " ")
    {
        overImage = 'no';
        setTimeout('mapOff2()',1000);
    }
}

// Stop hiding the code here -->
</SCRIPT>
```

This new line tells the engine to wait for 1000 milliseconds (1 second) and then call our second `off` function—`mapOff2()`. This interlude gives the user a chance to roll over another graphic before we unhighlight the images. If the user was simply moving between secondary categories on the submenu, there is no need to have the main navigation image flicker on and off. This will become clearer in the second `off` function, so let's get started on it.

Whenever the user rolls over an image, we are setting the value of the variable `overImage` to `yes`; we will use this variable to test whether or not we will turn off the highlighted image. Let's look at the first step in our `mapOff2()` function.

```
function mapOff2()
{
    if ((overImage == 'no') && (whichMenu != " "))
    {
        . . .
    }
}

// Stop hiding the code here -->
</SCRIPT>
```

Before we go ahead and turn off any of the images, we need to make sure that the user hasn't rolled over another image in the time it took to call this new function. We have set up an `if` statement to take care of that: If the variable `overImage` holds the value no and the variable `whichMenu` is not at its default value, then we can turn off any highlighted graphics. First, we will turn off the submenu graphic and return it to the default text blurb.

```
function mapOff2()
{
    if ((overImage == 'no') && (whichMenu != " "))
    {
        // revert to article's quote callout image
        document.submenu.src = "images/nav/
        sec_blank.gif";
        . . .
    }
}

// Stop hiding the code here -->
</SCRIPT>
```

This new line uses the same method that we have been using throughout the rest of the script, and the submenu should now be turned off with the original text blurb back in place. Next, we need to turn of the main navigation image that is currently highlighted.

```
function mapOff2()
{
    if ((overImage == 'no') && (whichMenu != " "))
    {
        // revert to article's quote callout image
        document.submenu.src = "images/nav/
        sec_blank.gif";

        // switch main nav. Image to
        // unhighlighted image
        eval ( "document." + whichMenu + ".src =
        'images/nav/" + whichMenu + ".gif'");
        . . .
    }
}

// Stop hiding the code here -->
</SCRIPT>
```

The final step in this function is to reset the `whichMenu` variable to its default value.

```
function mapOff2()
{
    if ((overImage == 'no') && (whichMenu != " "))
    {
        // revert to article's quote callout image
        document.submenu.src = "images/nav/
        sec_blank.gif";

        // switch main nav. Image to
        // unhighlighted image
        eval ( "document." + whichMenu + ".src =
        'images/nav/" + whichMenu + ".gif'");

        whichMenu = " ";
    }
}

// Stop hiding the code here -->
</SCRIPT>
```

We just finished our second `off` function. Now we need to create a navigation function that will send the user to the right URL when he or she clicks on the submenu secondary categories. Because there will be only a single image map that controls all seven submenus, we need to create a function that will look at which submenu is up and choose the right URL.

```
function goThere (sectionNum)
{
    if (whichMenu)
    {
        . . .
    }
}

// Stop hiding the code here -->
</SCRIPT>
```

Again, as with all of our functions, the first thing we need to do is check and make sure a category is currently selected—we wouldn't want to send the user somewhere if he or she accidentally clicked on the text blurb. Once we are sure a category is selected, we can then go about finding out where we need to send the user and then get him or her there.

```
function goThere (sectionNum)
{
```

```
if (whichMenu)
{
        subSection = section[whichMenu][sectionNum];
        location.href = whichMenu + "/" + subSection
        + ".html";
}
}

// Stop hiding the code here -->
</SCRIPT>
```

The first new line of code reaches into the array, grabs the name of the article's page and puts it into the variable sub-Section. Then the next line uses that variable, along with the value held in whichMenu, to set a new value for the location property of the DOCUMENT object.

As with the images, we are relying on the fact that each category's content is in a directory that has the same name as the section. For example, the article on "Supermodel Diets" in the Dirt section is located at dirt/supermodel.html. Again, this does save time in coding, but you must make sure that you have complete control over the naming conventions of the files.

Only one more step to go and we're home free: We need to insert the event handlers into the main navigation image <A HREF> tags, and then create the image map that controls the submenus and put handlers there as well.

Inserting the Event Handlers

Let's take a look at the <A HREF> tags for the main navigation and put the event handlers into them. Here's the code snippet for the main navigation images and the submenu/text blurb image.

```
<TABLE>
<TR>
<TD>
<A HREF="dirt/index.html"
onMouseOver="mainNavOn('dirt');" onMouseOut="mapOff();">
<IMG SRC="images/nav/dirt.gif" NAME="dirt" BORDER="0"
width="135" height="30" alt="Dirt"></A><BR>

<A HREF="money/index.html"
onMouseOver="mainNavOn('money');"
onMouseOut="mapOff();">
<IMG SRC="images/nav/money.gif" NAME="money" BORDER="0"
width="135" height="27" alt="Money"></A><BR>
```

```
<A HREF="trends/index.html"
onMouseOver="mainNavOn('trends');"
onMouseOut="mapOff();">
<IMG SRC="images/nav/trends.gif" NAME="trends" BORDER="0"
width="135" height="29" alt="Trends"></A><BR>

<A HREF="haute/index.html"
onMouseOver="mainNavOn('haute');"
onMouseOut="mapOff();">
<IMG SRC="images/nav/haute.gif" NAME="haute" BORDER="0"
width="135" height="26" alt="Haute"></A><BR>

<A HREF="street/index.html"
onMouseOver="mainNavOn('street');"
onMouseOut="mapOff();">
<IMG SRC="images/nav/street.gif" NAME="street" BORDER="0"
width="135" height="27" alt="Street"></A><BR>

<A HREF="profiles/index.html"
onMouseOver="mainNavOn('profiles');"
onMouseOut="mapOff();">
<IMG SRC="images/nav/profiles.gif" NAME="profiles"
BORDER="0" width="135" height="29" alt="Profiles"></A><BR>

<A HREF="columns/index.html"
onMouseOver="mainNavOn('columns');"
onMouseOut="mapOff()">
<IMG SRC="images/nav/columns.gif" NAME="columns"
BORDER="0" width="135" height="26" alt="Columns"></A><BR>
</TD>

<TD>
<IMG SRC="images/nav/sec_blank.gif" NAME="submenu"
BORDER="0" USEMAP="#submenuMap" width="287" height="221"
alt="Submenu">
</TD>
</TR></TABLE>
```

The onMouseOver event handlers should look pretty familiar, they are used in the same manner as those for our other rollover scripts. The onMouseOut handlers are slightly different in that we aren't passing a value to the function; this is because of the different way in which we are handling our rollovers. Also note that even though we are using an image map for the submenu/text blurb image, we still need to give it a NAME property in the <IMG> tag. Now, let's move on to the final event handlers: those inside the image map. This image map must contain four hot spots—one for each of the submenu options.

```
<MAP NAME="submenuMap">
     <AREA COORDS="11,66,110,82" SHAPE="rect"
     HREF="JavaScript:goThere(3);"
     onMouseOver="submenuOn(3);"
     onMouseOut="mapOff();">
     <AREA COORDS="10,48,58,63" SHAPE="rect"
     HREF="JavaScript:goThere(2);"
     onMouseOver="submenuOn(2);"
     onMouseOut="mapOff();">
     <AREA COORDS="9,31,71,44" SHAPE="rect"
     HREF="JavaScript:goThere(1);"
     onMouseOver="submenuOn(1);"
     onMouseOut="mapOff();">
     <AREA COORDS="9,10,84,26" SHAPE="rect"
     HREF="JavaScript:goThere(0);"
     onMouseOver="submenuOn(0);"
     onMouseOut="mapOff();">
</MAP>
```

We will need three event handlers in each of the hot spots. The `onClick` handler in the HREF field will call our `goThere()` function, which will handle sending the user to the proper location when an option is clicked.

The `onMouseOver()` handler is calling the `submenuOn()` function that will take care of highlighting the right image when the user rolls over an option. The values that we are passing to the function correspond with the positions of the entries in the second level of the multidimensional array we populated earlier. Finally, the `onMouseOut` handler calls our first `off` function—`mapOff()`.

Well, believe it or not, that's it! The arrays can get pretty large and cumbersome, but they make the coding much easier, and let you change data, such as links and section names, pretty easily. We covered quite a bit in this script, so let's take one last look at what we accomplished and how we did it.

REVIEWING THE SCRIPT

1. First, we created and populated the two variables `whichImage` and `overImage`, which we will need later in the script to keep track of what the user has rolled over.

2. Next, we defined and populated a multidimensional array to hold all of the information we would need to make the submenu system work.

```javascript
<SCRIPT Language="JavaScript">
<!-- Code after this will be ignored by older browsers

var whichMenu=" ";
var overImage = 'no'
section = new Array(4);

        section['dirt'] = new Array (4)
            section['dirt'][0] = 'supermodel'
            section['dirt'][1] = 'affairnet'
            section['dirt'][2] = 'moss'
            section['dirt'][3] = 'thrift'

        section['money'] = new Array (4)
            section['money'][0] = 'worldclique'
            section['money'][1] = 'germany'
            section['money'][2] = 'mergers'
            section['money'][3] = 'nmearnings'

        section['trends'] = new Array (4)
            section['trends'][0] = 'tshirts'
            section['trends'][1] = 'sweatshirts'
            section['trends'][2] = 'hats'
            section['trends'][3] = 'mugs'

        section['haute'] = new Array (4)
            section['haute'][0] = 'paris'
            section['haute'][1] = 'gaudy'
            section['haute'][2] = 'taffeta'
            section['haute'][3] = 'royalty'

        section['street'] = new Array (4)
            section['street'][0] = 'angry'
            section['street'][1] = 'prison'
            section['street'][2] = 'skater'
            section['street'][3] = 'hip_hop'

        section['profiles'] = new Array (4)
            section['profiles'][0] = 'moxon'
            section['profiles'][1] = 'west'
            section['profiles'][2] = 'trinidaddy'
            section['profiles'][3] = 'spurn'

        section['columns'] = new Array (4)
            section['columns'][0] = 'column1'
            section['columns'][1] = 'column2'
            section['columns'][2] = 'column3'
            section['columns'][3] = 'column4'
```

3. After we built our arrays, we created five functions we need to run our script.

The first function, `mainNavOn()`, takes care of turning off previously rolled-over main navigation images, as well as highlighting the new main navigation image and bringing up the proper secondary submenu image.

```
function mainNavOn (sectionName)
{
    overImage='yes';
    // make sure user already rolled over a
    // main nav image
    if (whichMenu != " ")
    {
        // unhighlight old section name
        eval ("document." + whichMenu + ".src =
        'images/nav/" + whichMenu + ".gif'");
    }

    // set variable to new rollover
    whichMenu = sectionName;

    // highlight the new image
    eval( "document." + whichMenu + ".src = 'images/
    nav/" + whichMenu + "_over.gif'");

    // bring up secondary navigation image
    eval("document.submenu.src = 'images/nav/" +
    whichMenu + "_sec_blank.gif'");
}
```

Next, we created the `submenuOn()` function, which determines which submenu is up and brings up the proper highlighted secondary category for that submenu.

```
function submenuOn (sectionNum)
{
    overImage='yes';

    if (whichMenu != " ")
    {
        // determine name of subsection
        // user is rolling over
        subSection = section[whichMenu][sectionNum];

        // swap out appropriate image
```

```
        eval("document.submenu.src = 'images/nav/" +
        whichMenu + "_" + subSection + "_over.gif'");
    }
}
```

The third and fourth functions share the responsibility for turning off the different submenu images when the user rolls off them. The first of the two, the mapOff() function, sets the overImage variable no and then uses a timer to call our second function after one second. The mapOff1() function then makes sure that the user is still not on a graphic and then turns off all of the highlighted graphics.

```
function mapOff ()
{
    if (whichMenu != " ")
    {
        overImage = 'no';
        setTimeout('mapOff2()',1000);
    }
}


function mapOff2()
{
    if ((overImage == 'no') && (whichMenu != " "))
    {
        // revert to article's
        // quote callout image
        document.submenu.src = "images/nav/
        sec_blank.gif";

        // switch main nav. image
        // to unhighlighted image
        eval ( "document." + whichMenu + ".src =
        'images/nav/" + whichMenu + ".gif'");

        whichMenu = " ";
    }
}
```

The goThere() function sends the user to the right URL when one of the image map hot spots is clicked on. It checks to see which main navigation category is selected, then goes into the array and pulls out the name of the secondary section it needs to send the user to, and sends the user there.

```
function goThere (sectionNum)
{
    if (whichMenu != " ")
    {
        subSection = section[whichMenu][sectionNum]
        location.href = whichMenu + "/" + subSection
        + ".html"
    }
}

// Stop hiding the code here -->
</SCRIPT>
```

4. Our final step was to add event handlers to the `<A HREF>` tags of the main navigation images, add the name property to the images affected by the rollovers, and then insert the necessary handlers into the image map that runs the submenus.

```
<TABLE>
<TR>
<TD>
<A HREF="dirt/index.html"
onMouseOver="mainNavOn('dirt');" onMouseOut="mapOff();">
<IMG SRC="images/nav/dirt.gif" NAME="dirt" BORDER="0"
width="135" height="30" alt="Dirt"></A><BR>

<A HREF="money/index.html"
onMouseOver="mainNavOn('money');"
onMouseOut="mapOff();">
<IMG SRC="images/nav/money.gif" NAME="money" BORDER="0"
width="135" height="27" alt="Money"></A><BR>

<A HREF="trends/index.html"
onMouseOver="mainNavOn('trends');"
onMouseOut="mapOff();">
<IMG SRC="images/nav/trends.gif" NAME="trends" BORDER="0"
width="135" height="29" alt="Trends"></A><BR>

<A HREF="haute/index.html"
onMouseOver="mainNavOn('haute');"
onMouseOut="mapOff();">
<IMG SRC="images/nav/haute.gif" NAME="haute" BORDER="0"
width="135" height="26" alt="Haute"></A><BR>

<A HREF="street/index.html"
onMouseOver="mainNavOn('street');"
onMouseOut="mapOff();">
```

```
<IMG SRC="images/nav/street.gif" NAME="street" BORDER="0"
width="135" height="27" alt="Street"></A><BR>

<A HREF="profiles/index.html"
onMouseOver="mainNavOn('profiles');"
onMouseOut="mapOff();">
<IMG SRC="images/nav/profiles.gif" NAME="profiles"
BORDER="0" width="135" height="29" alt="Profiles"></A><BR>

<A HREF="columns/index.html"
onMouseOver="mainNavOn('columns');"
onMouseOut="mapOff()">
<IMG SRC="images/nav/columns.gif" NAME="columns"
BORDER="0" width="135" height="26" alt="Columns"></A><BR>
</TD>

<TD>
<IMG SRC="images/nav/sec_blank.gif" NAME="submenu"
BORDER="0" USEMAP="#submenuMap" width="287" height="221"
alt="Submenu">
</TD>
</TR></TABLE>

<MAP NAME="submenuMap">
    <AREA COORDS="22,10,278,48" SHAPE="rect"
    HREF="JavaScript:goThere(0);"
    onMouseOver="submenuOn(0);"
    onMouseOut="mapOff();">
    <AREA COORDS="22,48,278,79" SHAPE="rect"
    HREF="JavaScript:goThere(1);"
    onMouseOver="submenuOn(1);"
    onMouseOut="mapOff();">
    <AREA COORDS="22,79,278,116" SHAPE="rect"
    HREF="JavaScript:goThere(2);"
    onMouseOver="submenuOn(2);"
    onMouseOut="mapOff();">
    <AREA COORDS="22,116,278,157" SHAPE="rect"
    HREF="JavaScript:goThere(3);"
    onMouseOver="submenuOn(3);"
    onMouseOut="mapOff();">
</MAP>
```

We have learned some new concepts in this chapter, and also enhanced our knowledge of concepts that we discussed in previous chapters. Let's take a look at what we covered:

- Multidimensional arrays and how to define, populate, and extract data from them.
- A new way to handle image rollovers.

RECAP

One look at the concept you put together for the homepage and the boss was sold. The script in this chapter is an example of just how far you can take JavaScript. We combined many of the elements from previous chapters to create a page that is truly on the cutting edge of Web programming. But don't think that this is the coolest or most complex application of JavaScript—far from it. With DHTML and stylesheets starting to gain popularity, the new features that are being added to JavaScript are truly amazing. We have come a long way and created some great scripts, even if they were for two fictitious companies. Now it's time to take what you have learned and use that knowledge to work on your own sites.

ADVANCED PROJECTS

1. Create a script that will randomly rotate a banner image and have each graphic go to a different URL.

2. Create a script that will set up a secure form submission by encrypting the data from the fields on a form.

3. Create a script to save user information data to a file on the Web server, so you can serve up a customized page when the user returns.

4. For Web sites that have lots of graphics on the homepage, create a splash screen and write a script that will load all of the graphics needed by the homepage, so the homepage itself will load quickly.

A Event Handlers

JavaScript is a language that is inherently event driven; that is, the scripts created in JavaScript usually are executed as a result of an event caused either by the user or the browser itself. We can harness these events through the use of event handlers. This appendix was created to give you a place where you can check out all of the different event handlers, their syntax, and a description of their uses.

◆ onAbort

Description: This handler is triggered when the user aborts the loading of an image, either by clicking on a link or hitting the Stop button.

Syntax: onAbort="code to be executed"

Implemented in: Navigator 3.0

Used within: Image

◆ onBlur

Description: This handler is triggered when a frame, window, or form element loses focus.

Syntax: onBlur="code to be executed"

Implemented in: Navigator 2.0/3.0

Used within: Button, Checkbox, FileUpload, Layer, Password, Radio, Reset, Select, Submit, Text, Textarea, Window

◆ onChange

Description: This handler is triggered when a Select, Text, or Textarea form field loses focus and its value is changed.

Syntax: onChange="code to be executed"

Implemented in: Navigator 2.0/3.0

Used within: FileUpload, Select, Text, Textarea

◆ onClick

Description: This handler is triggered when a Form object is clicked on or the handler is placed within an <HREF> tag and the image or text link is clicked on.

Syntax: onClick="code to be executed"

Implemented in: Navigator 2.0/3.0

Used within: Button, Checkbox, document, Link, Radio, Reset, Submit

◆ onDblClick

Description: This handler is triggered when a Form object is double-clicked on or the handler is placed within an <HREF> tag and the link is double-clicked on.

Syntax: onDblClick="code to be executed"

Implemented in: Navigator 4.0

Used within: document, Link

◆ onDragDrop

Description: This handler is triggered when the user drops an object, such as a file, onto the Navigator window.

Syntax: onDragDrop ="code to be executed"

Implemented in: Navigator 4.0

Used within: Window

◆ onError

Description: This handler is triggered when the loading of a document or an image causes an error.
Syntax: onError ="code to be executed"
Implemented in: Navigator 3.0
Used within: Image, Window

◆ onFocus

Description: This handler is triggered when a Window, Frame, Frameset, or Form element receives focus.
Syntax: onFocus ="code to be executed"
Implemented in: Navigator 2.0/3.0/4.0
Used within: Button, Checkbox, FileUpload, Layer, Password, Radio, Reset, Select, Submit, Text, Textarea, Window

◆ onKeyDown

Description: This handler is triggered when the user presses a key.
Syntax: onKeyDown ="code to be executed"
Implemented in: Navigator 4.0
Used within: document, Image, Link, Textarea

◆ onKeyPress

Description: This handler is triggered when the user presses a key.
Syntax: onKeyPress ="code to be executed"
Implemented in: Navigator 4.0
Used within: document, Image, Link, Textarea

◆ onKeyUp

Description: This handler is triggered when the user releases a key.

Syntax: onKeyUp ="code to be executed"

Implemented in: Navigator 4.0

Used within: document, Image, Link, Textarea

◆ onLoad

Description: This handler is triggered when all of the content is finished loading into a window or all of the frames within a frameset. It can also be triggered by the loading of an image.

Syntax: onLoad ="code to be executed"

Implemented in: Navigator 2.0/3.0

Used within: Image, Layer, Window

◆ onMouseDown

Description: This handler is triggered when the user presses the mouse button.

Syntax: onMouseDown ="code to be executed"

Implemented in: Navigator 4.0

Used within: Button, document, Link

◆ onMouseMove

Description: This handler is triggered when the user moves the cursor.

Syntax: onMouseMove ="code to be executed"

Implemented in: Navigator 4.0

Used within: None

◆ onMouseOut

Description: This handler is triggered when the user moves the cursor off the object.

Syntax: onMouseOut ="code to be executed"

Implemented in: Navigator 3.0

Used within: Layer, Link

◆ onMouseOver

Description: This handler is triggered when the user moves the cursor over the object.

Syntax: onMouseOver ="code to be executed"

Implemented in: Navigator 2.0/3.0

Used within: Layer, Link

◆ onMouseUp

Description: This handler is triggered when the user releases the mouse button.

Syntax: onMouseUp ="code to be executed"

Implemented in: Navigator 4.0

Used within: Button, document, Link

◆ onMove

Description: This handler is triggered when a script or the user moves the window or a frame.

Syntax: onMove ="code to be executed"

Implemented in: Navigator 4.0

Used within: Window

◆ onReset

Description: This handler is triggered when the user resets a form.

Syntax: onReset ="code to be executed"

Implemented in: Navigator 3.0

Used within: Form

◆ onSelect

Description: This handler is triggered when the user selects some text either from a Text or Textarea form field.

Syntax: onSelect ="code to be executed"

Implemented in: Navigator 2.0

Used within: Text, Textarea

◆ onSubmit

Description: This handler is triggered when the user submits a form.

Syntax: onSubmit ="code to be executed"

Implemented in: Navigator 2.0

Used within: Form

◆ onUnload

Description: This handler is triggered when the user exits the document.

Syntax: onUnload ="code to be executed"

Implemented in: Navigator 2.0

Used within: Window

B JavaScript Objects

Since JavaScript is an object-oriented language, and it's kind of hard to do much without knowing the objects supported in the language, we have decided to include this reference. This appendix breaks down the different objects in JavaScript into five different categories, and gives you the objects along with their properties and methods.

◆ Core Objects

The core objects are objects that aren't associated with the Java-Script object hierarchy and are available to both client-side and server-side applications.

Array

Description: An array is an object that lets you store sets of data, with each element of the data set stored in its own unique position, which in turn can then be referenced or retrieved.

Syntax for creating:

new Array(arrayLength); or
new Array(element0, element1, ..., elementN);

Parameters:

arrayLength—The desired initial length of the array.
elementN—This is the initial set of values that will be stored in the array. The array length will be set to the number of arguments.

Implemented in: Navigator 3.0

Properties: index, input, length, prototype

Methods: concat, join, pop, push, reverse, shift, slice, splice, toString, unshift

Boolean

Description: The Boolean object is used as a container for a Boolean value.

Syntax for creating: new Boolean(value)

Parameters: value—The initial value of the Boolean object.

Implemented in: Navigator 3.0

Properties: prototype

Methods: toString

Date

Description: The Date object gives you the capability to work with dates and times.

Syntax for creating:

new Date(); or
new Date("month day, year hours:minutes:seconds") or
new Date(yr_num, mo_num, day_num, hr_num, min_num, sec_num)

Parameters:

day, hours, minutes, month, seconds, year—If used, these various parts of the date will be string values.
day_num, hr_num, min_num, mo_num, sec_num, yr_num—If used, these various parts of the date will be integers.

Implemented in: Navigator 2.0/3.0

Properties: prototype

Methods: getDate, getDay, getHours, getMinutes, getMonth, getSeconds, getTime, getTimezoneOffset, getYear, parse, setDate, setHours, setMinutes, setMonth, setSeconds, setTime, setYear, toGMTString, toLocaleString, UTC

Function

Description: This object contains lines of JavaScript, which are executed when the object is accessed.

Syntax for creating: function name(arg1, arg2, ...argN) { functionBody }

Parameters:

arg1, arg2, ...argN—A set of string values that can be used to store data passed into the function. functionBody—The set of JavaScript commands to be interpreted by the function.

Implemented in: Navigator 3.0

Properties: arguments, arity, caller, prototype

Methods: toString

Math

Description: This object contains methods and properties that help in doing advanced math.

Syntax for creating: None—the Math object is a built-in part of the JavaScript engine and can be called or referenced without having to create it.

Implemented in: Navigator 2.0

Properties: E, LN10, LN2, LOG10E, LOG2E, PI, SQRT1, SQRT2

Methods: abs, acos, asin, atan, atan2, ceil, cos, exp, floor, log, max, min, pow, random, round, sin, sqrt, tan

Number

Description: This is an object that contains primitive numeric values. It is useful in dealing with numeric values.

Syntax for creating: new Number(value);

Parameters: value—This is the numeric value to be contained within the object.

Implemented in: Navigator 3.0/4.0

Properties: MAX VALUE, MIN VALUE, NaN, NEGATIVE INFINITY, POSITIVE INFINITY, prototype

Methods: toString

Object

Description: This is the built-in JavaScript object from which all objects within JavaScript are descended.

Syntax for creating: new object();

Parameters: None

Implemented in: Navigator 2.0/3.0
Properties: constructor, prototype
Methods: eval, toString, unwatch, valueOf, watch

RegExp

Description: This object contains a regular expression that can be used to find, replace, and manipulate matches in strings.
Syntax for creating: new RegExp("pattern", "flags");
Parameters:

pattern—The text contained within the regular expression.
flags—There are three possible values for a flag: global match(g), ignore case(i), both global match and ignore case(gi).

Implemented in: Navigator 4.0
Properties: $n, $, $*, $&, $+, &', $', global, ignoreCase, input, lastIndex, lastMatch, lastParen, leftContext, multiline, rightContext, source
Methods: compile, exec, test

String

Description: This object contains a series of characters that make up a string.
Syntax for creating: new String(string);
Parameters: string—A string.
Implemented in: Navigator 2.0/3.0/4.0
Properties: length, prototype
Methods: anchor, big, blink, bold, charAt, charCodeAt, concat, fixed, fontcolor, fontsize, fromCharCode, indexOf, italics, lastIndexOf, link, match, replace, search, slice, small, split, strike, sub, substr, substring, sup, toLowerCase, toUpperCase

◆ Document Objects

This section covers the Document object and all of its related objects.

Anchor

Description: This object contains a string that is the target of a hypertext link contained within an HTML page.

Syntax for creating: theString.anchor(nameAttribute)

Parameters:

theString—A string object.

NAME—A string that specifies a name.

Created by: Either the <A> tag in an HTML document or a call to the String.anchor method will create an Anchor object.

Implemented in: Navigator 1.0

Event Handlers: NA

Properties: None

Methods: watch, unwatch

Applet

Description: This object contains any Java applets contained within an HTML page.

Syntax for creating: NA

Created by: The HTML applet tag.

Implemented in: Navigator 3.0

Properties: All of the public properties of the applet are available through the object.

Methods: All public methods.

Area

Description: This object represents an area of an image map. For more information on its properties, see the Link object.

Implemented in: Navigator 3.0

document

Description: This object contains the properties of the current document.

Syntax for creating: NA

Created by: This object is created by the <BODY> tag of an HTML document as the runtime engine reads the page.

Implemented in: Navigator 2.0/3.0/4.0

Event Handlers: onClick, onDblClick, onKeyDown, onKeyPress, onKeyUp, onMouseDown, onMouseUp

Properties: alinkColor, anchors, applets, bgColor, cookie, domain, embeds, fgColor, formName, forms, images, lastModified, layers, linkColor, links, plugins, referrer, title, URL, vlinkColor

Methods: captureEvents, close, getSelection, handleEvent, open, releaseEvents, routeEvent, write, writeln

Image

Description: This object contains an image and permits access to the image's properties.

Syntax for creating: new Image(width, height)

Parameters:
> width—The width of the image.
> height—The height of the image.

Created by: The image constructor or an <IMG> tag found within an HTML document.

Implemented in: Navigator 3.0/4.0

Event Handlers: onAbort, onError, onKeyDown, onKeyPress, onKeyUp, onLoad

Properties: border, complete, height, hspace, lowsrc, name, prototype, src, vspace, width

Methods: handleEvent

Layer

Description: This object contains a layer from an HTML document and permits access to the layer's properties.

Syntax for creating: NA

Created by: Either the <LAYER> or <ILAYER> tag in an HTML document will create a Layer object.

Implemented in: Navigator 4.0

Event Handlers: onBlur, onFocus, onLoad, onMouseOut, onMouseOver

Properties: above, background, below, bgColor, clip.bottom, clip.height, clip.left, clip.right, clip.top, clip.width, document, left, name, pageX, pageY, parentLayer, siblingAbove, siblingBelow, src, top, visibility, zIndex

Methods: captureEvents, handleEvent, load, moveAbove, moveBelow, moveBy, moveTo, moveToAbsolute, releaseEvents, resizeBy, resizeTo, routeEvent

Link

Description: This object contains a link from an HTML document and permits access to the link's properties.

Syntax for creating: theString.link(href)

Parameters:

theString—A String object.

HREF—A string that specifies a URL.

Created by: Either the <A HREF> or <AREA> tag in an HTML document, or a call to the String.link method will create a Link object.

Implemented in: Navigator 2.0/3.0/4.0

Event Handlers: onClick, onDblClick, onKeyDown, onKeyPress, onKeyUp, onMouseDown, onMouseOut, onMouseOver, onMouseUp

Properties: hash, host, hostname, href, pathname, port, protocol, search, target, text

Methods: handleEvent

◆ Window Objects

This section covers the Window object and all of its related objects.

Frame

Description: This object contains a frame, which is specified in an HTML frameset. Every frame is, in reality, a Window object; the Frame object is just used for convenience.

Syntax for creating: NA

Created by: Either the <FRAME> or <FRAMESET> tag in an HTML document will create a Frame object.

Implemented in: Navigator 2.0/3.0

Event Handlers: See the Window object.

Properties: See the Window object.

Methods: See the Window object.

History

Description: This object contains an array that holds all of the URLs that the user has visited within that window.

Syntax for creating: NA

Created by: This is a built-in JavaScript object.

Implemented in: Navigator 2.0/3.0

Event Handlers: NA

Properties: current, length, next, previous

Methods: back, forward, go

Location

Description: This object contains the current URL.

Syntax for creating: NA

Created by: This is a built-in JavaScript object.

Implemented in: Navigator 2.0/3.0

Event Handlers: NA

Properties: hash, host, hostname, href, pathname, port, protocol, search

Methods: reload, replace

screen

Description: This object contains information on the display screen and colors.

Syntax for creating: NA

Created by: This is a built-in JavaScript object that the runtime engine creates.

Implemented in: Navigator 4.0

Event Handlers: NA

Properties: availHeight, availWidth, height, pixel-Depth, width

Methods: NA

Window

Description: This object delineates a browser or frame.

Syntax for creating: NA

Created by: This object is created by each <BODY>, <FRAMESET>, and <FRAME> HTML tag, or by the open method of the Window object.

Implemented in: Navigator 2.0/3.0/4.0

Event Handlers: onBlur, onDragDrop, onError, onFocus, onLoad, onMove, onResize, onUnload

Properties: closed, defaultStatus, document, frames, history, innerHeight, innerWidth, length, location, menubar, name, opener, outerHeight, outerWidth, pageXOffset, pageYOffset, parent, personalbar, scrollbars, self, status, statusbar, toolbar, top, window

Methods: alert, back, blur, captureEvents, clearInterval, clearTimeout, close, confirm, disableExternalCapture, enableExternalCapture, find, focus, forward, handleEvent, home, moveBy, moveTo, open, print, prompt, release-Events, resizeBy, resizeTo, routeEvent, scroll, scrollBy, scrollTo, setInterval, setTimeout, stop

◆ Form Objects

This section covers the Form object and all of its related objects.

Button

Description: This object contains a push button from an HTML form.

Syntax for creating: NA

Created by: The <INPUT> tag with "button" specified as the TYPE attribute.

Implemented in: Navigator 2.0/3.0/4.0

Event Handlers: onBlur, onClick, onFocus, onMouseDown, onMouseUp

Properties: form, name, type, value

Methods: blur, click, focus, handleEvent

Checkbox

Description: This object contains a checkbox from an HTML form.

Syntax for creating: NA

Created by: The <INPUT> tag with "checkbox" specified as the TYPE attribute.

Implemented in: Navigator 2.0/3.0/4.0

Event Handlers: onBlur, onClick, onFocus

Properties: checked, defaultChecked, form, name, type, value

Methods: blur, click, focus, handleEvent

FileUpload

Description: This object contains a file upload element from an HTML form.

Syntax for creating: NA

Created by: The <INPUT> tag with "file" specified as the TYPE attribute.

Implemented in: Navigator 2.0/3.0/4.0

Event Handlers: onBlur, onChange, onFocus

Properties: form, name, type, value

Methods: blur, focus, handleEvent, select

Form

Description: This object contains an HTML form and all of the objects contained within that form.

Syntax for creating: NA

Created by: The runtime engine creates this object when it comes across a <FORM> tag in an HTML document.

Implemented in: Navigator 2.0/3.0/4.0

Event Handlers: onReset, onSubmit

Properties: action, elements, encoding, length, method, name, target

Methods: handleEvent, reset, submit

Hidden

Description: This object contains a hidden Text object from an HTML form.

Syntax for creating: NA

Created by: The <INPUT> tag with "hidden" specified as the TYPE attribute.

Implemented in: Navigator 2.0/3.0
Event Handlers: NA
Properties: form, name, type, value
Methods: NA

Option

Description: This object contains an individual option from a selection pull-down menu.

Syntax for creating: new Option(text, value, default-Selected, selected)

Parameters:

text—Sets the text to be displayed in the menu list.
value—Sets the value returned to the server when the form is submitted with that option chosen.
defaultSelected—Sets the option that is initially true or selected.
selected—Sets the current state of the option.

Created by: The <OPTION> tag or the use of the Option constructor.

Implemented in: Navigator 2.0/3.0

Event Handlers: NA

Properties: defaultSelected, selected, text, value

Methods: NA

Password

Description: This object contains a text field from an HTML form that conceals its value.

Syntax for creating: NA

Created by: The <INPUT> tag with "password" specified as the TYPE attribute.

Implemented in: Navigator 2.0/3.0/4.0

Event Handlers: onBlur, onFocus

Properties: defaultValue, form, name, type, value

Methods: blur, focus, handleEvent, select

Radio

Description: This object contains a single radio button from a set of buttons on an HTML form.

Syntax for creating: NA

Created by: The <INPUT> tag with "radio" specified as the TYPE attribute.

Implemented in: Navigator 2.0/3.0/4.0

Event Handlers: onBlur, onClick, onFocus

Properties: checked, defaultChecked, form, name, type, value

Methods: blur, click, focus, handleEvent

Reset

Description: This object contains a Reset button from an HTML form.

Syntax for creating: NA

Created by: The <INPUT> tag with "reset" specified as the TYPE attribute.

Implemented in: Navigator 2.0/3.0/4.0

Event Handlers: onBlur, onClick, onFocus

Properties: form, name, type, value

Methods: blur, click, focus, handleEvent

Select

Description: This object contains a selection pull-down menu from an HTML form.

Syntax for creating: NA

Created by: The <SELECT> tag inserted into an HTML form.

Implemented in: Navigator 2.0/3.0/4.0

Event Handlers: onBlur, onChange, onFocus

Properties: form, length, name, options, selectedIndex, type

Methods: blur, focus, handleEvent

Submit

Description: This object contains a Submit button from an HTML form.

Syntax for creating: NA

Created by: The <INPUT> tag with "submit" specified as the TYPE attribute.

Implemented in: Navigator 2.0/3.0/4.0
Event Handlers: onBlur, onClick, onFocus
Properties: form, name, type, value
Methods: blur, click, focus, handleEvent

Text

Description: This object contains a text field from an HTML form.
Syntax for creating: NA
Created by: The <INPUT> tag with "text" specified as the TYPE attribute.
Implemented in: Navigator 2.0/3.0/4.0
Event Handlers: onBlur, onChange, onFocus, onSelect
Properties: defaultValue, form, name, type, value
Methods: blur, focus, handleEvent, select

Textarea

Description: This object contains a multiple input text field from an HTML form.
Syntax for creating: NA
Created by: The <TEXTAREA> tag.
Implemented in: Navigator 2.0/3.0/4.0
Event Handlers: onBlur, onChange, onFocus, onKeyDown, onKeyPress, onKeyUp, onSelect
Properties: defaultValue, form, name, type, value
Methods: blur, focus, handleEvent, select

◆ Browser Objects

This section covers the objects that contain the properties specific to the browser.

MimeType

Description: This object contains a MIME type supported by the browser.
Syntax for creating: NA

Created by: This object is automatically created when the browser is loaded.

Implemented in: Navigator 3.0

Properties: description, enabledPlugin, suffixes, type

Methods: NA

navigator

Description: This object contains information about the user's browser.

Syntax for creating: NA

Created by: This object is automatically created when the browser is loaded.

Implemented in: Navigator 2.0/3.0/4.0

Properties: appCodeName, appName, appVersion, language, mimeTypes, platform, plugins, userAgent

Methods: javaEnabled, plugins.refresh, preference, taint-Enabled

Plugin

Description: This object contains a plug-in installed on the user's browser.

Syntax for creating: NA

Created by: This object is automatically created when the browser is loaded.

Implemented in: Navigator 3.0

Properties: description, filename, length, name

Methods: NA

Index